E

F P

T O Z

L P E D

P E C F D

E D F C Z P

F E L O P Z D

D E F P O T E C

L E F O D P C T

F D P L T C E O

20/20 VISION

TRANSFORMING YOUR CHILDREN'S MINISTRY

Changing The World One Child At A Time!

Pastor Ray Baldwin
with **Nancy Baldwin**

20/20 Vision: Transforming Your Children's Ministry
by Pastor Ray Baldwin with Nancy Baldwin

©2023, SureWord Childrens Ministry LLC

ISBN: 979-8-9881116-2-7

Scripture quotations taken from the Amplified® Bible (AMP), Copyright © 2015 by The Lockman Foundation. Used by permission. www.Lockman.org.

Scripture quotations taken from the American Standard Version (ASV), Public Domain.

The Holy Bible, Berean Study Bible, BSB
Copyright ©2016, 2018 by Bible Hub
Used by Permission. All Rights Reserved Worldwide.

Scripture quotations are from The ESV® Bible (The Holy Bible, English Standard Version®), copyright © 2001 by Crossway, a publishing ministry of Good News Publishers. Used by permission. All rights reserved.

All Scripture marked with the designation "GW" is taken from GOD'S WORD®.
© 1995, 2003, 2013, 2014, 2019, 2020 by God's Word to the Nations Mission Society. Used by permission.

Scripture taken from the Holy Bible: International Standard Version®. Copyright © 1996-forever by The ISV Foundation. ALL RIGHTS RESERVED INTERNATIONALLY. Used by permission.

Scripture quotations taken from the New American Standard Bible® (NASB), Copyright © 1960, 1962, 1963, 1968, 1971, 1972, 1973, 1975, 1977, 1995 by The Lockman Foundation Used by permission. www.Lockman.org

Scripture quotations taken from The Holy Bible, New International Version® NIV® Copyright © 1973 1978 1984 2011 by Biblica, Inc.™ Used by permission. All rights reserved worldwide.

Scripture taken from the New King James Version®. Copyright © 1982 by Thomas Nelson. Used by permission. All rights reserved.

Scripture quotations marked (NLT) are taken from the Holy Bible, New Living Translation, copyright © 1996, 2004, 2015 by Tyndale House Foundation. Used by permission of Tyndale House Publishers, a Division of Tyndale House Ministries, Carol Stream, Illinois 60188. All rights reserved.

This book or parts thereof may not be reproduced in any form, stored in a retrieval system, or transmitted in any form by any means—electronic, mechanical, photocopy, recording, or otherwise—without prior written permission of the Publisher, except as provided by United States of America copyright law.

Printed in the United States of America

Sometimes it is the people no one can imagine anything of, who do the things no one can imagine.

—Alan Turing

Children's church is what shaped me to desire Kingdom culture. It created an expectation for the Holy Spirit to move in me and through me, and that my age does not put a limit on what He can do."

—**Stephen Harrison**
*StrikeForce General &
Knight KOG 'Emeritus'*

Children's ministry is probably one of the most rewarding jobs in the world, and I have never seen anyone put so much of their own blood, sweat, and tears in it as Ray and Nancy Baldwin have. There are so many people that are going to spend eternity in heaven because of Ray and Nancy's love for Jesus and children everywhere. I am honored to call them my friends.

—**Kornpop McCullough**
International Clown Ministry

Dedication Page

We dedicate this book to our own seven incredible grandchildren, the true love of our lives:

Jack, our seriously handsome actor and model, our first grandchild, who changed everything;

Kat, the strikingly beautiful red head whose love of music, and the classics constantly amaze us;

Anne, the agile joyous heart, whose "spark" for life shines through her irresistible smile;

Julie, whose has a heart for all creatures, great and small, especially if they are in need of rescuing;

Morgan, whose longboard and bicycle await to carry him from one adventure to the next;

Adeline and Isabella the extraordinary terrific twins, who wake us every morning with a smile, a "squidgy" (hug), and a simple request to watch *Frozen* for the umpteenth time;

plus the thousands of spiritual grandchildren we have received over the more than forty-five years of ministry;

and, to all the children and families whose lives are extremely precious to us, this book is for you and the multitudes of grandchildren yet to be added to the book being written in heaven.

Ray and Nancy
"Grampus and Nini"

Acknowledgments

More than twenty years ago, Nancy and I began to write down what we have learned over forty years of children's ministry. The idea of creating a book only came up in our wildest dreams. Many times, our oldest son, Austin, reminded us of the thousands of children's workers who would benefit from our insight and ideas. He, along with several others, encouraged us to write. Well, our book is finally here.

Writing down our thoughts and ideas, and presenting them in a book turned out to be more daunting than we ever imagined. Yet, as challenging as it was, the experience and rewards proved to be well worth the journey.

Dr. Cathy Block, we are eternally grateful, first, for your extraordinary love and hugs that you lavishly poured into our lives during this epic journey. You were indescribably patient with us as we worked out each chapter. For your expertise in writing, editing, sorting, and making sense of every chapter, we simply have to say that words are inadequate and lacking in expressing our gratitude.

Austin Baldwin, we can't thank you enough for the endless hours you spent adding your imaginative pre-edits and for the addition of your testimony.

Dr. Jeff Wickwire, thank you so much for your incredibly well-written foreword and your constant encouragement to write a book.

*Turning*Point Church (TPC), a heartfelt thank you for the love, trust, support and encouragement you constantly give us as we purposefully set out to *change the world one child at a time*, starting with your children.

The Knights of God (KOG or the Knights), without you, the children's ministry in The Castle at TPC would be so empty, so ordinary. You have impacted so many lives as you have grown and ministered to both young and old. Special thanks to each of the Knights, present and past, who added their testimonies to this endeavor: Meagan Benz, Rachel Van Lear, Sala Jewel, Carl and Gian Pedida, and Logan and Charlotte MacIntosh.

A special thank you also to Christie Gare (StrikeForce, East Texas), now a professional photographer in Frisco, Texas; and, Pastor Jared Ayres (StrikeForce, East Texas) now in youth ministry in College Station, Texas, for your testimonies.

Brenda MacIntosh (StrikeForce General) now in Denver, Colorado (CO) for your testimony and all you do for the Knights.

Special thanks to Majesty Champion Christian for being the greatest cover designer imaginable.

CONTENTS

Forward 14

Preface 17

CHAPTER 1
We're Not In Kansas Anymore 22

CHAPTER 2
Why I Am A Children's Pastor 34

CHAPTER 3
Why Do You Work with Children? 42

CHAPTER 4
Children In Revival 52

CHAPTER 5
The Castle 64

CHAPTER 6
God Is On The Move 80

CHAPTER 7
Please Sir, I Want More 94

CHAPTER 8
How to Begin A Children's Ministry, Part One 110

CHAPTER 9
How to Begin A Children's Ministry, Part Two 126

CHAPTER 10
How to Begin A Children's Ministry, Part Three 152

CHAPTER 11
If You Can Read, You Can Do Anything 170

Notes 188

About The Authors 191

FORWARD

I have known Ray and Nancy Baldwin for almost fifteen years. They have served as my children's pastors the entire time. Early on, I noted their genuine love and burden for children. I also witnessed their very unique approach to reaching them. They are the real deal!

In this fantastic and imminently helpful new book, *20/20 Vision*, they have drawn richly from their decades of children's ministry. Included in its pages, you will find the wisdom from their own rich experience, as well as testimonies from those who have played a part in reaching children with them. And, you will also hear from the former participants who were wonderfully touched by their ministry as children. This is one of the great strengths of the book. I love testimonies!

As a church, we regularly hear from pastors and Christian workers around the world who are trying their best to reach children but haven't been able to land on the proper template or approach. If you are one of them, this book is tailor made for you. I urge you to read slowly and take notes. Ray and Nancy cover all you need to know to launch a successful children's ministry with helpful, practical, hands-on instructions.

My prayer is that God will use this wonderful book to encourage children's workers everywhere. And that new children's ministries will be launched that effectively reach the children of this generation, whose souls are now under so much concentrated attack from the enemy!

Dr. Jeff Wickwire
Senior Pastor & Founder of
Turning Point Church

PREFACE

Being true to the mission, I do not dilute or pollute the truth, which is always in the very forefront of my mind as I prepare each day for battle against our enemy. I suit up with God's armor every morning. I fill my hands, heart, mind and spirit with God's Word, and after having met personally with the Lord for much needed encouragement and guidance, I feel adequately prepared for whatever may lay ahead of me when I venture out of my front door (and even sometimes before I venture out).

I make my way to ground zero—our local elementary school. One may be inclined to think I am greatly exaggerating my role as a children's pastor, and that for the most part it's really not that big a deal. If so, then perhaps your understanding of the role of a children's pastor needs reshaping.

Never before in church history has there been a more clarion call for men and women to teach, train and disciple all of our youngest saints in the faith. The battle to gain access to the hearts and minds of the children of our King has been in full swing since Adam took his first breath. From then until now, the enemy has pulled no punches in his all-out, no-holds-barred effort to turn the hearts of the heirs of heaven against the truth of their Father's love.

For centuries, the body of Christ has mistakenly operated

Preface

in the understanding that children are often smelly, loud, uncomfortable baggage, accompanying the much needed, capital-carrying wallets of adult parishioners. As such, they must be volleyed into closets and pacified with the latest, most affordable curriculum in hopes that some of them will see the need to take up their crosses, and become the much needed, capital-wielding adults who value the church in their futures. This perspective has been a critical, tactical error and our enemy has seized upon it.

We, the church, have allowed our most valuable assets—the most moldable, pliable, precious resources on the planet—to be stolen from right under our righteous-elevated noses, because we didn't see the opportunity, or the need, to actively prepare these energetic, vibrant young believers to become the most powerful forces in the universe.

Years ago, Nancy and I realized the tactical advantage that the forces of evil had over our children. I heard the Holy Spirit say in my heart, "It is imperative that we reach, teach, and disciple the children who are occupying the damp beige-colored, dimly-lit recesses of our churches if we are to secure the future of the church." The six- to twelve-year olds, who sit around eight-foot tables, on metal folding chairs, coloring poorly copied Bible pictures with broken crayons, are not the church of tomorrow as most think. They are the church of today, who are being ushered down a path of boredom, and into the roles of those Ken Ham calls "The Already Gone."

We need to see more clearly. We must understand and accept our great commission with more clarity and urgency. We need the perfect 20/20 vision of God to see and be seen the way God sees. I cry out daily that my eyes may see just as Elisha prayed in 2 Kings 6:17 (ESV):

> O Lord, please open his eyes that he may see. ...;

and as recorded in Psalm 119:18 (NLT):

> Open my eyes to see,
>   the wonderful truths in your instructions.

The story that unfolds, as you turn the pages of this book, records the journey that Nancy and I are taking to fulfill the vision God has given us to change children's ministry. This book describes our steps toward creating a viable, energetic program where children can be reached, taught and discipled into becoming a part of the powerful, unmovable church of the loving God.

As you read, you will find that we take our calling very seriously, because we are reminded of what Jesus said in Matthew 18:6 (NIV):

> If anyone causes one of these little ones—those who believe in me—to stumble, it would be better for them to have a large millstone hung around their neck and to be drowned in the depths of the sea.

I'm not a great swimmer so I make it my goal in life to stay far away from the deep end of God's judgment.

Each and every child needs the opportunity to meet Jesus for themselves, to make their own choices to follow Him, and not to be assimilated into a spiritual stupor by the latest, poorly presented, state-of-the-art miscommunication of what Christianity is. In Matthew 19:14 (NIV):

> Jesus said, "Let the little children come to me, and do not hinder them, for the kingdom of heaven belongs to such as these."

Preface

How will "little children" come to Jesus unless someone specifically goes out of their way to introduce them to the Savior (Matt 19:14)? How will they come to the Savior unless someone is convinced of the importance of taking the message of God's love to them? These are the souls who have limited understanding of His love. They have not seen much of life's experiences, and they still may even believe in Santa Claus.

"Can a child really get saved?" one pastor asked.

My answer was, and is a resounding, *"Yes!"*

"How do you get children to receive a personal relationship with the Lord?"

Great question. I will answer it in "Chapter Nine: How to Begin A Children's Ministry, Part Two."

Earlier, you read about my allusion to the battlefield. My battlefield is our local elementary school. If you don't believe that it is a battlefield, ask your elementary school principal for their assessment. This is where children assemble and spend most of their childhood days. It's the perfect place to reach, teach, and disciple children. Yet, I know what you are thinking: "How can we do this in public schools?" It isn't as difficult as you think. Check out the chapter entitled, "If You Can Read, You Can Do Anything".

Nancy and I have spent a lifetime working with children, and for many years, have felt the need to write down our experiences, victories, and failures. At the urging of our senior pastor, Dr. Jeff Wickwire, and many others, we have written this book. We pray that it will not only bless you, but also challenge you to rethink your children's ministry. We pray that it will enable you to make your children's ministry relevant to the needs of today's church and today's children.

Changing the world one child at a time,
Ray and Nancy Baldwin

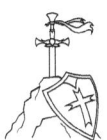

The days of Sunday school need to be over. ... Only in recent years has a new and innovative way to reach young, eager minds for the Lord arisen. It has emerged out of the sheer necessity to actually redeem this generation from spiritual disaster.

Chapter One

WE'RE NOT IN KANSAS ANYMORE

In 1780, the owner and editor of the *Gloucester Journal*, Robert Raikes, started his first school for children. It began for boys in the families of chimney sweeps in Sooty Alley, Gloucester (England), with girls being allowed to attend several years later. This school was located right across the street from the city prison. They met in the home of a Mrs. Meredith.

The original daily schedule, as written by Raikes, was:

> The children were to come after ten in the morning, and stay till twelve; they were then to go home and return at one; and, after reading a lesson, they were to be conducted to Church. After Church, they were to be employed in repeating the catechism till after five, and then dismissed, with an injunction to go home without making a noise.[1]

Robert Raikes was described as warmhearted and flamboyant. Through his newspaper, he advertised his "new idea." After his first editorial appeared in 1783, his schools spread with astonishing rapidity. In 1785, the Sunday School

Society was established to organize and coordinate this new program for the poor children in northern England. In that same year, in Manchester and Salford, alone, there was said to be close to 1,800 students attending "school" every Sunday.[2]

Portrait of Robert Raikes, founder of Sunday school, by George Romney.

During this period, throughout Northern England and Wales, it was quite common that both adults and children attended these classes. Even after enduring vicious opposition, by 1831, Robert Raikes's "Sunday schools" were reaching and teaching almost 1.25 million English children. That number equaled almost 25 percent of the population.[3]

I wholeheartedly commend these pioneering children's ministers of long ago. Their ideas and efforts reached so many and in so many ways.

I've heard it said, that if you continue to do what you have always done, expecting different results, then you might be bordering on foolishness. For years my wife, Nancy, and I have spent our lives teaching and training children in the United States. We have also traveled to several countries sharing the good news of a different approach to the 1700–1800s model of children's Sunday school.

We have talked to both children and adults. Throughout all our years of doing this, we have noticed that one thing has stood true: the world is full of foolishness when it comes to doing what we need to do to reach the children of our world. Let me explain.

For a couple hundred years, the church followed, like sheep, the efforts of a man who created a tool and a machine designed to educate the poor, working children of the eighteenth and nineteenth century. Because these children worked eighteen-

Chapter One

hour days, six days a week, they did not have the opportunity to receive any type of education except on Sundays. Due to these limitations, Raikes created what he called "Sunday school" to not only educate the working white slaves of England, but also give them a decent meal and bath.

Children from local communities came from all over to attend these classes. Their curriculum was simply a Bible. Hundreds and thousands of children and many adults where taught to read and write in these "Sunday schools" during the industrial revolution. Through these classes, many also found faith in God, which opened the door to a spiritual revolution. As children and adults learned to read, they also learned about God, heaven, creation, angels, miracles, and yes, Jesus. Their minds were educated, and their hearts changed.

Eventually the church got on the bandwagon and said, "Hey, this Sunday school is a great way to educate our kids about God. I know it has worked for many decades."

This new "Sunday school" idea also began to catch on widely with evangelicals. Two in particular were Hannah and Martha More. They were sisters who lived in Mendip Hills (southern England). Their schools went beyond Raikes's original design. They included innovative ideas to help children learn, created classes that were grouped by ages, and adapted instruction for children who were at different levels in their education. When children's attention spans began to wane, they even went as far as to insert energetic songs and music into the lessons. These sisters also professed that, in order to achieve the best results,

Statue of Raikes in the Victoria Embankment Gardens, London.

it might be advantageous to be kind to the children.

Their battle cry was: "Train up a child in the way he should go and when he is old he will not depart from it" (Prov 22:6 NKJV). They started training classes and called them Sunday school. Eventually, every week, churches all over the world held Sunday school classes for all ages, including adults. And so, Sunday school was birthed.

Much the Puppet teaches with Nancy's help.

After some time, huge printing and publishing companies were called upon as a cry rang out for more curriculum, better curriculum, and more powerful curricular approaches to reach today's families with the precious Word of God. Sunday school publishing became a big business. It exploded with products ranging from workbooks, coloring books, puzzles, prizes, and later, in more modern times, records, cassette tapes, videos, DVDs, puppets, full-body characters, other types of illusions, and all manner of fancy, eye-catching gadgets. Each one was designed with the modern child in mind. These curricula were marketed as having been tried, tested, and proven to work.

Every September, new and innovative creations hit Christian bookstore shelves. Every year, new children's seminars and conferences sprang up all over, each crammed with vendors doing everything they could to sell their wares to frustrated, and often depressed, children's workers. These workers were desperately seeking a new way to reach the now almost unreachable, unteachable, and hardened children in our modern world's local churches.

I know, I said, "... now almost unreachable, unteachable, and hardened children in our modern world's local churches."

Chapter One

Let me ask you a question. If you were a child today, would you attend your church? I have a catch phrase I use a lot: "We are not in Kansas anymore!"

This is no longer your grandmother's church. We must find a way to take hold of the ever-growing imagination of the modern child, who has been deeply affected by outside stimuli, that is far more exciting and compelling than anything the church has been offering.

Consider this: the child of today is not the same animal as the child Robert Raikes encountered in 1780's England. The modern day child has been bombarded with "stuff"— TV, movies, video games, Disney World, computers, iPads, iPods, iPhones, and every other electronic gadget available to man. Every day, the news is filled with both horror and hate. Today, simply by watching the news, sitcoms and soap operas, and by playing the most descriptive video games filled with violence, foul adult language and situations, most kids have had a concise, adult education long before they reach the age of ten. They are bombarded with information from every possible direction.

Moreover, when these same ten-year-olds attend school, they are expected to learn content in their elementary school courses that you and I didn't even cover in high school. By the time they reach high school, they are taking courses that were once only given to third-year university students. The child of today is not the same child you were at the same age. What reached you *will not* reach today's child.

Why do we continue to do the same old thing, not gaining any ground, but rather continuing to lose more and more ground? Why are we so hell-bent on using what has not worked in decades, in hopes that it might possibly work, if we only buy the next, newest gadget, or try harder and pray more diligently?

Little Johnny

Take the life of an average ten-year old boy today. He is a child of a broken home, or he simply lives with his single mom who works every hour she can just to make ends meet. He gets up early every Monday morning, eats breakfast—if he's lucky—and runs to catch the bus for an hour long ride to school. The bus driver yells, "Sit down, and be quiet." He arrives at school and his teachers tell him, "Sit down, and pay attention."

For seven hours that day, he does everything he can to not only stay awake and pay attention, but also to get an education. At the end of the school day, he gets back on the bus and rides for an hour. Upon his arrival at home, he quickly shucks his coat and school books, and heads toward the door and the outside world. However, his mom tells him, "Get your homework done before you go play or watch television." For the next couple of hours, he labors to finish up so that he might have a little free time to be what he is: *a child*.

Then, it's off to bed early because it's a school night, and the whole process starts all over again early the next day. For five days every week, he rises early, and goes through this ritual to gain what his parents and teachers hope for: an education.

Do you suppose this little guy really enjoys going to school every day of the week, working a couple of hours or more every night with homework, and then doing more "school" on the weekend too? Ah, the weekend! A time when Johnny can get out of the weekly grind and go run, play, and have adventures with his friends! But no, along comes church.

Johnny gets an invitation to attend church. Mom, dad and the church hope, and pray that Johnny will find Christ and become a godly man. These aspirations are placed, with high expectations, in the time-tested program called Sunday school. This "school" starts early on Sunday mornings where children

Chapter One

are asked to come dressed in their "Sunday best." They are also asked to sit in cold, beige-colored rooms with oversized, metal chairs around a well-worn table. The teacher, who may or may not want to be there, tells the children who show up, "Please sit down." They ask them to pay attention for the next sixty minutes while they cover all the material that the Sunday School Superintendent expects them to teach.

Their battle cry is: "Johnny, we want you to come to Sunday school today." Do you know what Johnny heard? He heard the word "school" and nothing else. He doesn't want to go to "school" again for the sixth day of every week. (Quick thought: school to children is their job, and to them its "work.")

The very last thing Johnny wants to do is come and sit in yet another class on a day he is supposed to be resting. Johnny is thinking, "Didn't God say that this was a day of rest?"

Let me ask you the same question I have asked hundreds of adults all over the world: how would you like it if after working five days a week, eight hours a day, and going home to work another two hours every evening, if you were asked, and expected to go back to work on Sunday mornings, but this time you were supposed to do it for free?

Right. That's what I thought.

Johnny isn't the only child who feels the same way that you just felt. More children than most of us care to imagine are already tired of church and Sunday school. Even children who regularly attend are "already gone" in their minds. They have decided that at the very first opportunity they have, they will leave Sunday school (church) and never return.

To the average child (of today), the stories about God, Jesus, and the Bible are simply that, just stories, fables, fairy tales, and, the stuff adults tell children to keep their young, imaginative minds alive, and to control them through guilt and authority.

The days of Sunday school need to be over. They must

pass into history, and honestly, they need to stay there. Only in recent years has a new and innovative way to reach young, eager minds for the Lord arisen. It has emerged out of the sheer necessity to actually redeem this generation from spiritual disaster. Children's Church and Children's Ministry have taken their place, and stepped up to the plate in today's modern churches. Now instead of Sunday school teachers, there has arisen from the heart of God a species of super humans called children's pastors/ministers.

Let me ask you, if there were a better way to reach our generation of children, would it be worth your time to check it out? Wouldn't it be better to first introduce Johnny to Jesus, and then tell him about the book God has written for him? Wouldn't this be a better approach than attempting to cram tons of mindless information into his brain every weekend at Sunday school? Wouldn't it be better than just continuing to do what hasn't been working successfully for decades, in hopes that someday or someway, perhaps on his own, Johnny would come to realize that Jesus loves him and he would turn his life over to God?

I'm sorry but this time-tested, centuries-old model of a typical Sunday school approach has failed miserably and in epic proportions. If it had worked, we would not have so many young people wandering about the world in a religious stupor. We would not have moms and dads who no longer attend church because of the efforts of well-meaning churches, who taught "religious education" to them when they were children, instead of reaching their hearts with the love of God.

As I write this, I am painfully aware that the church is failing. She is dying, and no one seems to know what to do or who to call, as we fall on our knees and cry out to God for revival. We are just one generation away from total spiritual annihilation. It is time that we change our tactics and start doing what works to reach kids like Johnny. The message of

Chapter One

God's love will never change, but the packaging must, or we will become the last generation left to read the obituary of the body of Christ to a lost and dying generation.

A New yet Old Idea

We found a new way to be extremely effective in reaching children and training them in the way they should go. Actually, it's not as new a method as you might think. The model we use can be found throughout the Scriptures.

Every time I say reaching and training, I really mean disciplining children to become a part of the vibrant, charismatic body of Christ, equipped to reach and train future generations for Christ.

Are you ready to learn what has become so blatantly obvious to so few churches?

First, what is the way they (today's children) should go? They should learn to love God with all their hearts, and become active ministers of the Gospel.

Second, how do we get them to learn this? We must show them the true and living Christ; and introduce them to a loving Father, and let them form a lasting relationship with Him.

Third, what do we do with them when they have learned this? We must teach and train them in ministry.

How we answer these three, important questions for all our children is found in the rest of this book. We'll begin answering these questions by looking at why children's pastors/ministers began children's ministries. In Chapter Two, I will explain why I became one! After reading my story, my prayer is that you will decide to join me.

Before we leave this chapter—and throughout this book—we want you to hear the stories of children and their parents who have experienced our children's church. We want you to learn the value of this new method of reaching today's children from these participants' perspectives. We will end all of our chapters with an unedited, unprompted testimony from someone who has, or still is, involved in *Kidz-Turn*, our children's church. We judge that their experiences will give you a bird's-eyes view into what it is like inside our mission to *change the world one child at a time*.

Testimony of Christie Gare

I have a very vague memory of when I went to Sunday school. I do remember it was a more formal setting and that it was not something I enjoyed. I only went because I and my siblings were supposed to go while my parents went to Sunday school with their friends. Later, Pastor Ray started children's church. It was *fun*. I vividly remember some of the songs and lessons that we had to this day, thirty plus years later. I remember the atmosphere and the exciting lessons with music, visual aids, and stories. Pastor Ray and Miss Nancy, as we called them, set up the children's church with an amazing forest feel and everything to match. There were no videos, just songs and lessons carefully prepared and studied. It was obvious that they took their work very seriously; it wasn't just an afterthought.

Another testimony as to how effective children's church was occurred when I "graduated" to middle school and had to go to a traditional Sunday school with other middle schoolers. I quickly found how boring and distant 'Sunday School' really was to my life now. In fact, after a few weeks, I remember that instead of continuing to go to "Sunday school" I went back to children's church to "help" with the kids. This decision led to such an impactful time for me. I was even given some responsibility which helped me to grow in leadership, and gave me new ideas on how to present the Gospel. It also enabled me to grow in my faith. I have fond memories of helping with

Pastor Ray's and Miss Nancy's children's ministry during my middle and high school years.

—Christie Gare
Former Member of Kidz-Turn

BEGIN THE CHANGE NOW

If you are a children's pastor and you are experiencing the ineffectiveness of your Sunday program, and need to change your approach in order to truly reach, teach and disciple your children, earnestly seek the Lord's guidance. Then, seek out the counsel of other children's pastors who are successfully discipling their kids. Draw up a plan of action to revitalize your ministry, and schedule a meeting with your senior pastor.

Describe why you feel your Sunday school may no longer be effective in reaching and grounding your church's children in their faith. Share your thoughts about the changes you would like to see. Ask your senior pastor what changes he or she might like to add to accomplish this goal. Be open to receiving your pastor's guidance and advice. With your pastor's blessing, you are free to begin.

If you are a parent, we will suggest several steps you can take to change the world one child at a time, beginning with your child(ren)! Some will be more difficult for you than others. We know this. We know you may modify some to fit your family's needs. We encourage you to take action on each recommendation, even if you have to take a "baby step" at first to build them into your lifestyle. We support you as you venture forward for your child(ren)'s benefit. Thank you.

To begin, think about how you felt about your Sunday

school experiences. Reflect on the experiences your children are having at your church. Does your child have an up-to-date relationship with the Lord? Do you agree that changes are necessary to improve your children's experiences with Christ?

Prayerfully consider becoming an active participant in your church's children's ministry. Assess how many hours you can realistically and totally invest to help make a difference in your church's children's spiritual lives.

Second, if you don't already have a family worship time in your home, create one. You can begin by scheduling a fifteen to twenty minute time in which the family comes together to read the Bible, worship and pray. Soon, you can alternate who selects the Bible verses to discuss, or who leads the worship and prayer time. Your children's abilities to lead these activities will grow through this time, opportunity, and support.

Chapter Two

WHY I AM A CHILDREN'S PASTOR

I met Jesus in 1971 when I was nineteen. We met in a small, Nazarene Church in Manchester, England. I never entered a church before, except for the occasional community "Bring-and-Buy Sale." It is safe to say that my life was an absolute mess. So as to not glorify this mess, I won't go into details except to say, if I had not given my life to Christ that night, I would not be alive today.

To say I was ignorant of spiritual things is an enormous understatement. Truthfully, I was overwhelmed by it all. In the beginning, I struggled. Many times I fell in my walk because of what I learned, and what I didn't know.

I remember telling my dad what had happened to me the night that I got saved. His answer was, "I'll give it a fortnight." Actually, it didn't last that long! In just a few days, I was out living my old life again. It was only through the persistence of the church's youth leader that I even made it through the first week. And, in my ignorance, I was ready and willing to prove my father wrong. Only God knew my heart. He was ready and willing to help me.

Before I met Christ, I had already left school at age fifteen. I entered the work force and the world, not knowing that there was so much more to life than what I was experiencing. At nineteen, I knew I had to learn more about this Jesus! So, twice a week, I was sitting in my church's Bible study with a couple of other young people. Every time I read a scripture, my mind filled with ideas that I never had before. I was so unaccustomed to them—living for Jesus instead of me; what a concept.

Still not understanding very much of what I read or heard, I wanted to find answers to the many questions that continued to arise from these biweekly studies. Then, one Sunday morning I was asked by the godliest man I knew what I thought about attending a Bible class at what was then British Isles Nazarene College. I remember laughing at his question, thinking he couldn't be serious. I was totally uneducated, and there was absolutely no way that I would ever make it to, or in, college. This godly man, Dr. Jack Ford, was the president of British Isles Nazarene College; and, he was serious!

I must have looked really strange to him as I laughed him off, but he continued. He asked me to come to his office the next evening. Strange as it seemed, I went. Dr. Ford was waiting, pen in hand, and with several sheets of questions on a desk. He asked if I would take an entrance exam to see if I was qualified to even attend the college. All I could think of was the last test I had taken in school, which I totally flunked. That was my reason for leaving school at fifteen!

For two hours, I sat and tried my best to answer each and every question. I knew I was not doing well, but he sat there in his overstuffed chair, sipping his tea and reading a book. With a smile on his face, he would sneak glances to see how I was doing. This made me feel like I really was in the wrong place! What was I thinking sitting in a room with this silver-haired, old man, attempting to look as if I knew anything worth writing down?

When I finished, I handed the test over, and made a hasty

Chapter Two

retreat to the bus stop. Two days later, I received word to come back to the college, and again, for reasons unknown to me, I went back. Dr. Ford was ecstatic! He shook my hand, and said, "Welcome to British Isles Nazarene College."

The next three years were pretty incredible. I grew more than I can say. Need I mention that some of my lecturers were not sure I would ever make it to graduation. I wondered about it myself almost every day! My home church was the essence of my support and strength. Every time I went, there was always an encouraging word and warm hug.

One lady in particular, Miss Tighe, was a source of tremendous strength. I could hear her words of wisdom and love throughout these many days of hardship echoing in my spirit. When things got difficult, she somehow always knew what to say. She would remind me that God had placed a call on my life, a call I knew nothing of yet, but through her warmth I gained strength.

My last year in college brought another big change. I married Nancy, the girl of my dreams! She has now been my wife for more than forty-four years. In addition, during that last year, I served on our church's board as youth director and ran a coffee house called "The Cove."

After graduation, Nancy and I decided to take a six-month trip to Iowa to meet her family. I would intern under her pastor, Reverend Dwayne Houston, at the Church of The Nazarene in Chariton, Iowa. I preached several times. Nancy and I sang a lot, and we taught our first children's church. It

> **Side Note**
>
> I read that this once bustling church (Iowa), teaming with both adults and children in the seventies, is now up for sale due to lack of attendance. Their message of holiness to the next generation may now be silenced. They fell to the sad, inevitable outcome that befalls every church who fails to "relevate" and repackage their message to an ever changing world.

was here, at this church, that we realized how God wanted to use us.

At this time, people began to tell me, as they will likely repeat often to you if you accept God's calling to work with children: "Don't waste your education on children."

Charles Haddon Spurgeon once said that the children he observed had much deeper and more intense experiences with God than most of the adults he knew.[4] I have to agree. It is no wonder people are so unnerved when they see the impact of God upon children—they have no grid with which to compare it! They have never had their own experiences with God, and so they cannot possibly relate to what is happening to children.

With this in mind, if you feel called to work in a children's ministry, you and I have a powerful opportunity in our grasps. If we are ever to change this world for Christ, we need to throw ourselves completely and whole heartedly into ministering to our children. It's time to bring the children's ministry from the back room to the forefront of the church. No more babysitting, pacifying, and crafting our kids into oblivion!

They have had enough of Sunday school and classes, games and snacks!

They want and need *God*!

The old adage, "Children should be seen and not heard," is *wrong*! Instead, I keep hearing the words of Jesus: "Forbid them not, to come unto me" (Matt 19:14 ASV).

It's time to move, *now*!

Our classrooms, hallways, playgrounds, and fields are ripe unto harvest like never before. Our children are crying out for something real. If we don't show them a real and *awesome* God, then the world will convince them of a fake and powerless existence.

Never before have we seen the move of God as we are right now on the lives of the young church of today. Children are standing, sitting, kneeling, weeping, and worshiping our Lord in every service. I stand and watch in awe as these young saints find the presence of God, their Father, and their lives are changed forever.

Adults weep as they experience the powerful and mighty presence of God that they feel in our children's services. They are amazed as they too are drawn into this heavenly place. We are seeing children moving in the Spirit as they begin to minister to one another. Children, who have never experienced Christ, are laying their lives at His feet for the first time as they share with others who are moved by God.

Our children's ministry has exploded with excitement and expectation. The numbers of children attending have grown exponentially with the swelling of God's love being poured out.

Ask yourself this question: if I don't minister to our children, who will?

It's time that we change the world one child at a time.

Testimony of Austin Baldwin

Austin, our son, is now the Chief Safety Officer on one of the world largest oil rigs in the Gulf of Mexico; a Wilderness First Responder in Montana; and, co-pastor in children's ministry at Journey Church in Bozeman, Montana.

Cairns [a Scottish word for a conical heap of stones built as a landmark] and trail signs. That's what it's like being the son of a pastor. You learn to read cairns and trail signs, and you learn them well (even more so when your father is a pastor to children). Confused? That was my intention. You see, we learn best when we're outside the known, beyond our comfort zone and a little off balance. Welcome to the life of a children's pastor's kid (CPK). Not a "PK" (pastor's kid), but a "CPK".

Now, before you think I'm voicing some sort of grievance with all this "off balance" and "confused-out-of-my-comfort-zone" talk, let me first say that the life of a kids' pastor's son is a constant Peter-in-Neverland existence. And yes, I had a mother along with dozens of other church ladies "assisting" as honorary grandmothers. There was also a band of "lost boys" in tow anytime I was in mischief, and there were plenty of deacons and elders to be Captain Hook following these said "mischiefs."

But, back to cairns and trail signs. My father is a master navigator of life, more specifically, the Christian life. (This is arguably the only real life, but I make the distinction here for the sake of inclusion). Dad started me off, as any apprentice woodsman and navigator should, right at his side. I had a desk next to his and a matching three piece suit to boot. I had all the trappings and gear right from the start!

When my father prepared his sermons (he started out as a senior pastor and graduated to children's ministry), I was always involved. When I would ask questions, he would answer in his own words and then guide me to C.S. Lewis, Corrie ten Boom, Larry Norman and, most importantly, the Bible. In this way, my didactic learning was forged. I was beginning to learn the maps and gain the tools that would help me navigate my Christian life. Now, the wheels had to go on the wagon.

Part of growing up a CPK means you never have to volunteer for anything. You were already volunteered in utero! I had no shortage of experiences in path clearing for summer camps, teepee set-ups for overnight camp outs, trash pickups following Sunday services, and the hosting of many, many missionaries and their families. Such frequent and varied experiences also gave me no shortage of opportunities to put my hands on and apply what my teacher, my Pastor, my father, had taught me. It was magic. Not always easy, but always magical. As I grew, dad would from time to time have to "correct" my navigation. He would show me where I had, by intent or lack thereof, missed a "trail sign" or completely walked over a "cairn" and subsequently lost my way. This of course gave me many occasions to question his teachings and guidance, but master navigators and woodsmen do not become so without many experiences of their own. I would find each time that he had been right all along and he had corrected my path.

Now as an adult, I continue to find the trail and markers much the same, neglected at times, but still the same. Each time I'm faced with a decision, confronted with an obstacle or just a little "lost," I look around for the cairn that is marking the way. Whether it's a verse I've not read in some time, an author whose writing I need to peruse, or the need to simply write or call my mentor, my pastor, my dad and get back on the trail of life and carry on. Also now, as a father, mentor, and pastor to my own little family (and my children's church), I have come to find these cairns and trail signs invaluable. I am teaching them to my own apprentices. I can only hope to be as good a mentor, pastor and dad as I have had.

Thanks, Dad.

—Pastor Austin Baldwin
Our first children's church member

BEGIN THE CHANGE NOW

If you are a children's minister, share your story of how you were saved, and why you became a children's pastor with the children at your church. Explain to your children what it feels like when God talks to you, in a way that they understand. Teach your children that they may hear a voice speaking to them, an uneasy feeling when they are about to do something that doesn't feel right, or the added feeling of joy that they can accomplish something that they might not have felt that they could do. Follow your talk by asking parents and their child(ren) if they have felt God calling them to do something and what the results were.

If you are a parent, share with your child(ren) a time when you felt called by God to be about His work. Describe how you felt. Ask your child if they have ever had an uneasy feeling in their stomach, such as a feeling that God was telling them not to do something. Ask how they felt when they listened to this feeling. What was the result? Then, ask if they have ever felt like they should do something and they did it. How did that feel? What was the result? Then, ask them to describe how it feels to them when God is talking to them.

Chapter Three

WHY DO YOU WORK WITH CHILDREN?

There is a simple answer why I work with children: God *told me* to work with children. There is also a more extensive answer that will take me a little longer to share. It involves several instances where children have proven to be the most moldable, pliable resource we have in the world today. Let me explain.

I vividly remember when I was nineteen years old, fresh off the streets of Manchester, England, standing in the fourth row of a tiny, seemingly insignificant church, watching. I was listening as the "pillars" of the church lead us in prayer on a cold, autumn Wednesday evening. No more than fifteen people attended this church, and I was now one of them. (It's a long story so I will cut to the chase.) Most of the church attendees were in their late sixties and seventies, leaving just three of us in our late teens. One by one our little congregation stood to pray.

Words that I never heard before rolled off their tongues with great ease. I noticed that they started on the front row, and each person along the row stood to pray, with no one being passed over. Then, they were on the third row. I suddenly realized that there were only three more people ahead of me before it would be my turn. I never prayed out loud before ... in front of people! My heart was racing and my mouth became as dry as a bone.

"What do I do?" As I stood trembling, my mind turned to mush. I was speechless.

It seemed like an eternity until I opened my mouth. Then I said, "Jesus, I love you."

From that moment on, I learned about "thirty seconds of prayer," a prayer whereby you tell Jesus how much you love him. Don't ask for a thing. He already knows what you need, as confirmed in Matthew 6:7-8 (NIV):

> 7 And when you pray, do not keep on babbling like pagans, for they think they will be heard because of their many words. 8 Do not be like them, for your Father knows what you need before you ask him.

Now after forty years, we still teach children to pray with these simple words: "Let's take about thirty seconds, and tell Jesus just how much we love him; speak loud enough for you to hear yourself." Every day in our children's church, as worship comes to a close, we lead children into this prayer. Why? Because children need to learn how to pray.

After that first, initial, four-word prayer in that little, Manchester church, I asked if someone could teach me how to pray like they did. Miss Tighe (the wonderful older lady I told you about before) told me that the prayer I prayed was perfect. She went on to say that I should always pray that way.

Over the years, I have read books on prayer—corporate prayer, intercessory prayer, conversational prayer, and the list goes on. I'm not accustomed to saying long prayers, or using words that are not only hard to pronounce, but also difficult to understand. On that day, when I asked Miss Tighe to teach

Chapter Three

me how to pray, she also gave me the best advice on prayer that I have ever received. She said: "Just be yourself."

I love to pray, and I truly enjoy teaching children to pray. The most rewarding experience a children's pastor can have is to just listen during the portion of worship when children are praying. Just standing and hearing little voices talking to the most high God, no petitions are made, no desperate pleas for help, just words of love spoken to their loving Savior and friend. Some kneel; others lie completely flat on the carpet. Many stand, but all pray.

For example, I once overheard the prayer of a child; he told Jesus how much he loved Him, and how thankful he was for his mom, who looked after him and brought him to church on her only day off. Another prayed and sobbed, as she literally hugged Jesus with her arms tightly wrapped around herself.

Over the years, Nancy and I have learned to never underestimate the prayers of a child. Let me share a few with you that have touched our hearts.

Patrick was just six when he asked us to help him pray for a daddy. Nancy told him that we would be honored to help him pray for a daddy. Patrick interrupted and said, "No, not just any daddy. I want to pray for *my* daddy". So, per his request, we added our agreement to Patrick's prayer for his real daddy. Immediately, as this six-year-old began to pray, Nancy and I had tears in our eyes. We were hearing one of the most passionate prayers for a dad that we had ever heard.

Later that day, Patrick's mom (who had just moved from Iowa to Tyler, Texas) told us that she had gotten pregnant while living in California, and had not seen Patrick's father since. This man didn't even know that he was a father.

Weeks passed; every Sunday, Patrick could be heard praying that same prayer. Shortly after his seventh birthday, he and his mom were shopping at the local Walmart when something very amazing took place. His mom walked around an end cap when she literally bumped into a young man: *Patrick's daddy.* Shocked and surprised, she just stood there in astonishment. He shared that two months earlier, he had been promoted in his firm. He found out that he would be moving from California to Tyler.

All this happened around the time Patrick began to pray. I would love to have been there as he was introduced to his daddy for the first time. I know you're wondering what happened to them. After several months of getting to know each other, and his daddy getting saved, Patrick's parents married. *A child's prayer was answered.*

• • •

Brandi was just seven when she heard her grandmother screaming from the porch of their lake home. Tornado sirens began to wail on what had been a beautiful Sunday afternoon just moments before. Brandi was playing in the water more than fifty yards away. She quickly ran to find "her Gemma" terrified as she looked down the lake at the very large, angry tornado that ravished the homes all along Lake Tyler East.

Later that day when they came to our home, Brandi's grandmother shared what had happened next: "I was terrified that we would be killed. I'm sure that I repeated my terror over and over several times."

Brandi, however, stood very calmly. She said, "Gemma, today Pastor Ray told us about how Jesus stopped the storm on the lake. I'm going to ask Him to stop this one, too."

Her grandmother was beside herself as Brandi stopped, looked right into the storm and said, "Jesus, you know that I love you, please save my Gemma and her house. Please stop this tornado from hurting anyone." Then, Brandi stomped her foot and shouted, "Tornado, stop now in Jesus's name."

"There, Gemma, it's gonna be alright, Jesus is taking care

Chapter Three

of it," announced Brandi.

To her grandmother's total surprise, the storm began to wane. The tornado turned into the lake and stopped. *A child's answered prayer saved lives.*

• • •

Tiffany was nine when her mother found her in her bedroom, crying tears of joy before Sunday lunch was served. She had gone to her room as soon as she had arrived home from church. She immediately slumped down beside her bed and began to pray. When she didn't come to lunch, her mom went to get her. Standing outside the bedroom door, she heard Tiffany talking to someone. She listened as Tiffany prayed.

When her mom asked Tiffany about her prayers later, Tiffany explained that she had heard from the Lord. He told her that if she would spend time every day praising and praying, He would do something very special through her. Days turned into weeks, and Tiffany spent more and more time with the Lord in prayer. One day she called me. She told me that Jesus had promised that if she were to lay her hands on children who were sick, He would heal them. It didn't take more than a day or so until the first person she prayed for was healed—a twelve year old with diabetes that had come to children's church and asked for prayer.

Tiffany sprang to her feet, laid hands on her, and the girl was instantly healed. This healing, according to her parents, resulted in their daughter no longer needing to get daily insulin shots.

Later, a little boy with half-inch thick glasses came forward and his crossed eyes became straight after Tiffany prayed for him. His older sister fainted as she watched it happen. There are so many accounts of Tiffany's healings; it would take forever to share them all. *A child's prayers healed others.*

Why Do You Work with Children?

•   •   •

Day four of Summer Fun University (SFU), our week-long summer camp, came to a close with our customary practice of giving time for children to pray for one another. Each afternoon, during our worship time, I would feel a tug on my shirt from the same seven-year old. Once again, she asked: "Pastor Ray, is it okay if I go and pray for the children?"

My response remained the same, "Yes, of course."

That day, I watched as she stepped around those had already been prayed over. She headed purposely to children who were still waiting, watching, and hoping for God to touch their hearts. It was as if she followed a higher power guiding her, and her little friend to exactly the right child.

Gently, she would stop, and ask if she could pray for each child that she felt called to address. Each bowed their heads, and closed their eyes. Then, she took their hands and raised them high above their shoulders. Then, a soft, Richter scale-registered prayer flowed from her heart. In just moments, she released their hands and touched their foreheads. Almost every time the same thing would happened; the power of God took over and the child being prayed for ended up in the arms of her friend, who then gently laid them on the carpet where they would stay for several minutes or longer. Then, off the girl would go to pray for another child, achieving the same result.

I wondered where she learned to pray this way, with such anointed power. However, I knew where it came from.

For those who know me, as a children's minister, I very rarely pray by laying hands on children unless they ask me to personally pray for them. Not that I don't want to pray for children, but I feel it's my calling to *teach* children how to minister to each other. To illustrate, a little girl watched the Knights—the older children who lead our worship services—pray for children many times. She witnessed how these children's lives had changed as a result. Each of the Knights had learned how to pray, and were now mentoring others on how to pray, intercede, and minister.

Why do you want to work with children? Seeing their prayers raised to, and answered by their loving Father is only one of the thousand, unmatched joys you will be blessed to witness every day if you work with children in children's church. Come see us in The Castle, the large auditorium we built as a castle in which we hold our children's church at TPC. I promise your life will never be the same again.

Testimony of Pastor Jared Ayers

It's difficult to express my gratitude for Pastor Ray in a few simple words. How do you talk about someone who has had such an impact in your life? When I go back to my earliest memories of childhood, he was there. In all of my life, I've never met someone with a bigger heart. To say that he loves what he does would be the greatest understatement of all time. Children's ministry is who he is at his core. His passion to see the next generation move the gospel of Jesus forward is unmatched. I owe so much to Pastor Ray.

One thing that I admire about him is the amount of time, energy, and resources he puts into developing young leaders. Children's ministry was never a stepping stone to "the next thing" for Pastor Ray. He understands the value of empowering kids to serve God and live passionately for Him. I memorized the books of the Bible under his leadership. I got into music because he taught us to love "praise and worship" times. I was filled with the Holy Spirit in children's church. I gave my heart to, and ultimately, fell in love with Jesus as a young kid. I was baptized by Pastor Ray. The list goes on. Without a doubt, I would not be where I am today if it wasn't for the guidance, leadership, and sheer commitment of Ray Baldwin.

Now, nearly twenty years later, I'm a pastor in College Station, Texas. Guess where I preached my first sermon—in Pastor Ray and Miss Nancy's children's church! I'll never forget the investment that Pastor Ray put into me. Because of him, I have the great privilege of standing on a stage and leading people to Christ every Sunday today. It all started because Pastor Ray saw something in this little boy who had no idea what God would do through his life. For that, I am humbled.

I can remember it all like it was yesterday. I also remember when was in third grade. I saw Pastor Ray and Mrs. Nancy roaming the halls of my school with that purple puppet named Much. I was so proud to say to all my friends: "That's my pastor!" That's the thing with Pastor Ray. Ministry doesn't stop at the stage in church. Reaching kids has always been his mission and it's evident by the way he lives his life. From summer camps to puppet shows, from Bible studies to learning how to pray, my life and my love for God and all His people would be impossible without the undying love and guidance of this man.

Even now, following his ministry though social media, I see myself reflected in the videos and photos of the kids. If they only knew how lucky they were to have such an incredible pastor and mentor. Leaders of his caliber are rare. I thank God that I had the privilege to have Pastor Ray and Mrs. Nancy in my life. There is no possible way of knowing the impact that they've had on Heaven. I know I am one of many whose lives were forever changed. The trajectory of my life all started with a bearded man and his guitar, a woman and her purple puppet, their faithfulness toward their calling, and their relentless pursuit of raising up a generation to love God and people.

—**Pastor Jared Ayers**
Youth Pastor at Sky Break Church
College Station, Texas

Chapter Three

BEGIN THE CHANGE NOW

If you are a children's minister, model the thirty-second prayer. Teach children how to pray just loud enough for them to hear themselves. Build this prayer time into your weekly worship services. Explain why it is important to learn how to pray aloud so that they can pray for others when the Holy Spirit calls.

If you are a parent, explain to your children how you learned to pray. Tell them why praying is important. Move beyond praying memorized prayers with them, such as "Now I lay me down to sleep … ." Pray with them at least once a day as they begin to nurture their own personal relationship with the Lord.

Children in our children's church also prophesy and minister God's Word to children and adults alike. This is awesome! No words can describe it.

Chapter Four

CHILDREN IN REVIVAL

If we don't teach our children how to pray, minister, move under the direction of the Holy Spirit, then we will end up raising a generation of needy, entitled, weak Christians, who have no idea about, or inclination to address, anyone else's needs but their own. Moreover, they would not know how to "bear one another's burdens …" (Gal 6:12 ESV).

Proverbs 22:6 (NKJV) plainly states that we must:

> Train up a child in the way he should go,
> And when he is old he will not depart from it.

Every worship service and lesson I teach is laced with training on how to minister to those around us, and how to defend our faith and beliefs. I know Jesus did the very same thing with His disciples and followers. He had sent them out into towns and villages to minister the truth of God's love, with incredible earth-changing results.

We train the Knights, not only to lead in worship, but also to minister and pray. In turn, they teach and train the next, younger generation of our children's church. As evidenced during our 2019 SFU, we have seen the fruits of this training.

It is my intention to leave a well-oiled, strong, and capable legacy of seasoned, spiritually strong giants of faith, who will step out and change the world one child at a time.

Simply stated—and if you were not already certain of this fact—when a child learns to pray, things happen in God's Kingdom. Look at the Bible for further confirmation. At a very early age, while he ministered to the Lord in the temple, Samuel had learned to pray. What would have happened if Samuel had never learned to pray and hear from God?

Unfortunately, we don't hear much about the effects of a child's prayer. I believe this is partly because we don't expect much from our children spiritually. We buy iPods, iPads, and video games to occupy their minds instead of teaching them to pray (by example), or buying them a Bible of their own to read. We send them to children's church while the adults go to church, or stay at home, in hopes that someday our children will remember what they heard as a child, and make the right choices as adults. We need to get on board, and train our children in the things of God (Prov 22:6, author's paraphrase).

Throughout history, there are many accounts of the lasting effects of a child's prayer. On many occasions, John Wesley wrote that during his travels he would come across a house filled with children praying.[5] As another example, in the 1800s, during the great Scottish revival, children could be heard weeping loudly during prayer services, not wanting to leave when it was over, and going straight home only to enter their prayer closets to continue praying.[6]

It is also said that more than half of the one million converts that Dwight L. Moody saw over his lifetime were children.[7] After his revival meetings, it was reported that thousands of children would walk for hours to attend all night prayer meetings.[8] Many of these prayer meetings were started and lead by children.[9]

I have heard this saying more than once in my life: "Children should be seen and not heard." How wrong is that? If you have ever been anywhere at the south end of TPC during

Chapter Four

praise and worship in The Castle, you will know that I don't believe that statement.

Children should be encouraged to pray. When taught to pray, children can, and do become very passionate prayers. They are able to reach the ears of their Heavenly Father. It is time we learned about this virtually untapped power of a child who loves God, and believes wholeheartedly in God's promises.

Children who visit us just once leave with a new heart and a rejoicing spirit ready to return next week for more. Once, an unsaved mother, who felt the need to leave the anointing of the adult sanctuary, hoping to hide amongst the fun of the children's church, unaware of the move of God among the children, was moved to tears during the ministry time with the children. She could not leave our service without making her decision to follow God.

Children even take their faith to school with them. I have watched several children pray for their friends and peers in their schools. They bring them to church, and in the anointed atmosphere of our children's church, it only takes one visit to introduce them to Jesus.

> "... out of the abundance of the heart, the mouth speaks" (Matt 12:34 NKJV).

In The Castle, children six to twelve years old fall on their knees during praise and worship, interceding for the lost, and praying for revival to sweep over the country. Some of the children have shared with Nancy and I that they wake up praying and interceding. As one parent shared with us, she walked into her daughter's room only to find her crying before the Lord. Her daughter was only eight years old. According to her mom, this depth of devotion and spiritual prayer happens on a daily basis.

During worship, many of our children feel it best to simply

kneel and worship. They do not pay any attention to those around them. You can hear them as they lift their voices before the Lord.

Children in our children's church also prophesy and minister God's Word to children and adults alike. This is awesome! No words can describe it. I find myself simply walking through the groups of children and adults, assisting were I can, as the children minister the love of God to one another. I watch as they lay hands on children and then adults; it is one of the most blessed experiences on earth to witness the effects of fervent prayer from a child who is praying for the adults before them, who stand much taller. It is equally powerful to observe children praying for the sick, or praying and interceding for the needs of others. All of their actions end with tremendous earth-shattering results.

John 14:12 is our most popular Bible verse. Many of our children have not only memorized, but have referenced it so often that their Bibles automatically fall open to that verse with the least amount of effort.

> "I tell you the truth, anyone who believes in me will do the same works I have done, and even greater works, because I am going to be with the Father" (John 14:12 NLT).

An eight-year-old girl came to me one day, and told me that she had a dream where thousands of sick people all waited in a line. As she watched them, she heard God's voice say directly to her: "If you will lay your hands on them and pray, they will be healed." When I asked her what she thought, she replied: "I believe that God wants me to pray for the sick, and they will be healed."

As I laid my hand on her and prayed for her, she immediately fell under the power of God. She laid on the floor well after the end of service, and the children had all but gone home. Later, her parents came in and helped her to her feet. At eight, she had been anointed to pray for the sick, and prayed earnestly every time we had anyone come for healing.

Experiences like this are now commonplace. Every service seems to be consumed by prayer, praise, and wonder. Before, we would end our services by playing a game, or doing Bible "Shoot-Outs" until the adults came to pick up their children. Not any more. Now the adults interrupt the children's service. After the adults have been dismissed from the Sanctuary, they arrive at children's church only to find the children ministering together, and to each other. Many are on their knees, or lying on their faces before the Lord. Many of their parents just stand and wait, silently encouraging their child(ren) as they have a moment with God.

The move of God among our children has been taking place for many years during our children's services. I wrote about it in an article[10] more than ten years ago:

> Not long ago some of the adults just sat in the hall so they too could enjoy the anointing as it flows out into the halls. At a recent C.A.R.E. Group meeting for the children (Cell Groups) when the parents came to pick up their children, the children did not want to leave, "Just a little longer, Mom, please" was the comment that I heard from a six-year old. The Mom agreed and both stayed in the Children's Church.
>
> A few weeks ago during a baptism service … [thirteen] children and [two] adults were baptized and the Spirit of God fell on the waters. As the children stepped into that very cold baptistery (the heater was not working for some reason), the Spirit of God became very evident.

After the service ended, many commented that they were moved to tears as they witnessed the children being baptized. Specifically, they were stirred when certain children entered the water. I had never experienced anything like this outpouring before!

After the baptismal ceremony ended, the Senior Pastor and I were still in the water, unable and unwilling to leave the pool. The doors between the baptistery and the sanctuary closed, yet we still stayed in the water praying and praising God. My wife was held to the wall of the ladies changing area for over one hour as she heard the voice of God telling her to simply, "Listen to what I have to say." She did not emerge from that room until the very end of the service, well over an hour later. She said that she had tried to leave several times only to be pushed back against the wall by God's power.

Several children visited the adult service last week. During the ministry time, one of our intercessors (a child of [ten]) began to pray with such fervency that many adults came forward. She laid hands on them and prayed for their needs. This anointed ministry is happening more and more in both the adults' and the children's services at our church.

My closing thought for this chapter is that we do what we know, until we know something different.

One day, a child asked me why people do dumb things. I asked for more specifics.

"My little brother is always getting into trouble because he doesn't obey the rules and talks back to mom a lot," she said.

Chapter Four

I simply told her, "We do what we know, until we know something different."

She looked a bit bewildered, so I took it a little further. I asked if she remembered when her little brother was a baby, before he could walk. Did she recall how all her brother could do was crawl around? That was all he knew how to do. Although he saw other people walking around upright on two feet, or saw them running, jumping, and dancing, all he knew to do was crawl. Then, after a while, because of his incredible capacity to learn and grow, he learned that he, too, could stand. Then, he took his first steps. Now, he knew something new.

"Does he still crawl around?" I asked.

She replied, "No, only when he's playing on the carpet with his cars."

I continued, "He did what he knew, until he knew something else."

I remember when Nancy and I read stories to our sons because they didn't know how to read. They both listened intently, enjoying every page, even though one was four years younger than the other. They were doing what they knew to do until they knew something different—how to read for themselves.

We both remember the day our oldest son, Austin, asked if he could read to us. We were elated as he carefully stumbled through each word. Although they still enjoyed hearing us read to them, they both found that there was even more to be enjoyed when they learned to read for themselves.

After Austin read to us, he began reading to Geoffrey, and the cycle continued. They did what they *knew* until they knew something *different*.

I know this is a simplistic explanation of growth, and each of us must travel along our own growth paths. Imagine if, as babies, we never learned to feed ourselves, walk, or talk. Imagine what we would have been like if we remained in the baby stage. Truthfully, it is not possible to do this and survive. Without growth, we would perish.

A Christian growing in Christ is just as important as growing into adulthood. The day of my second birth was incredible for sure. I knew at that moment I was a new person. I knew my sins were forgiven. I knew if I died that day, I would be ushered into God's presence to take my place in heaven.

> 12 Whoever has the Son has life; whoever does not have the Son of God does not have life.
> 13 I have written these things to you who believe in the name of the Son of God, so that you may know that you have eternal life (1 John 5: 12–13 NIV).

That was all I knew, and yes, it was enough for the time being. However, I noticed that there was more to being a Christian, so much more. I watched others begin to immerse themselves in God's Word. I saw their love, joy, strength, and desire to share their faith with others. I witnessed the depth of their relationship with God, the Father, and with other Christians. So I began to grow in Christ. I learned new things every day—or rather "changed" with every new nugget of knowledge.

If we are not changed when we learn, then we did not learn.

> Therefore leaving the elementary teaching about the Christ, let us press on to maturity, ... (Heb 6:1 NASB).

> Instead, we will speak the truth in love, growing in every way more and more like Christ, who is the head of his body, the church (Eph 4:15 NLT).

Chapter Four

As a children's pastor, I am in a unique situation where I get to witness children learning and changing all the time. What I find fascinating are the looks on their faces when they learn something new. It changes their hearts and the way they live. They move from the baby stage as Christians into a deeper, stronger, more loving relationship with Christ. Even a child in Christ does what they know to do until they know something different.

I'm paraphrasing Maya Angelou: "Do the best you can until you know better. Then, when you know better, do better."[11] We teach our children to "do better" by Scripture journaling. We teach them:

Don't just read Scripture.
Say it.
Write it.
Remember it.

Testimony of Meagan Benz

Yes, The Castle is my favorite room in the entire church, even now! The Castle is this fairy-tale, sacred place that all the kids get to go to on Sundays. I just remember feeling so honored and so welcomed walking in its doors. It is a real life castle and I sometimes didn't want to leave! Just reminiscing of my time spent there brings out the child-like spirit in me. Yes, this amazing place was a ton of fun, but I also grew so much in my time there. I didn't just learn about Jesus and the Bible, but I learned how to create my relationship with God and grow in it.

I learned how to pray and really mean it. My prayers weren't just some scripted words that I had to say before meals or bed anymore. It was what I did when I wanted to talk to a friend. I remember Pastor Ray giving us a time to just sit after his talk or worship and pray if we wanted. This was the first time

I experienced the Holy Spirit. I don't remember what I prayed that day, I just remember getting this feeling. A feeling of joy because I knew I wasn't alone. I left that Sunday and I haven't lost that feeling since.

The Castle was the first place where I really worshiped God. I wasn't just singing words to a fun song; I was singing to, and for, Him. These words meant something. All of this set the stage for my entire life. I had no idea at the time. The way I learned to worship was built over time. Pastor Ray believed in me and gave me the opportunity to step out of my comfort zone. I sang on The Castle stage alongside some others that I admired. I even got to sing on stage in the adult sanctuary during our Christmas production. This created a ripple effect in my life because I had found something that I loved to do.

I went on to help lead the worship time in my Youth group. Even now at my college, I lead worship with a high school ministry called "Young Life." In The Castle, I learned that my favorite way to connect to God was through praise and worship. This discovery has affected my daily adult life and spiritual relationship ever since. This children's ministry did more than just teach me Bible stories and songs. It taught me how to grow and how to live a full and abundant life, loving my Lord Jesus Christ.

—**Meagan Benz**
Former member of Kidz-Turn

Chapter Four

BEGIN THE CHANGE NOW

If you are a children's minister, have you heard your children weeping loudly during prayer services, not wanting to leave when it was over, and only going straight home to enter their prayer closets so that they could continue praying? If so, this is a sign that your children are in revival. If this is not occurring, begin asking your children to take thirty seconds to thank God for all He has done in their lives. Ask them to lift their voices to the Lord, loud enough for them to hear their own voices. Also, teach your children to "Scripture journal." It will build their spiritual lives.

If you are a parent, and you have not recently seen that wonderful look on your children's faces when they have learned something new about the Lord, about their own spiritual growth, or if they are not leaving their worship services with a new heart, and a rejoicing spirit ready to return next week for more, ask your children's minister if they would read this book. Also, talk with your children about the new joys they are receiving in their walk with Jesus. Teach them to write these new joys in their Scripture Journals, that you show them how to make.

Parents arrive at the end of our service only to find their little ones completely engrossed in the presence of the Holy Spirit, having their young lives being changed and impacted. I could write another book filled with so many exciting testimonies of God's power to change young lives.

Chapter Five

THE CASTLE

Nancy and I are so thankful for the opportunity to work with so many awesome, young people! We are blessed to have the honor of planting good seeds into their hearts and minds every day. Then, we witness their growth in Christ and the strengthening of their relationship with Him.

We would like to share just a few moments-in-time from The Castle. The Castle is "the castle" where we hold our children's church. We offer these glimpses into our ministry so you can experience, vicariously, what days are like in ministry with children.

A Day in The Castle Kidz-Turn

Before I share the schedule of a typical day in our children's church, you might want to know about the lessons that I teach. I write all the curricula. It has been my privilege to write The Castle curricula for over a decade.

I predominately teach in series. There are just a few weeks in the year where I insert what I call a "Onezie." These are lessons with a theme for a special day, i.e., Valentine's Day where I teach on "Perfect Love," or "I am Loved;" and, on All Saints Day, I have taught "Let's Start A Jesus Revolution," or "I'm Just A Kid, Can God Use Me?" Some of the series we have covered over the last few years include:

- "I Am One of Them";
- "Making Jesus the Most Famous Talked about Person on the Planet";
- "Children and the Supernatural";
- "Jesus, The Unstoppable";
- "The B.I.B.L.E.— Basic Instructions Before Leaving Earth";
- "Jesus in Me Makes Me Shine";
- "Keep Calm, God's Got This";
- "There's Gotta Be More";
- and "Let's Talk About Fear."

What follows is a typical day and service schedule in The Castle, or at least what we plan, until the Holy Spirit steps in and makes adjustments. Our church has multiple Sunday morning services. The Castle services are approximately seventy minutes long, and start five minutes after the adult services, or "big kids church." This allows for late arrivals, and gives a few minutes for our kids to enjoy each other's company as they get acquainted.

A five-minute countdown becomes visible on the main screen. As it reaches one minute, the cups, balls, and video games are quickly stowed away for the next service. As soon as the timer ends, a loud, vibrant, exuberant music video begins and serves as a call to worship. Within moments the video has drawn every child to the floor. Most dance, sing, and enjoy praising and worshiping together with old and new friends. Some children, who are either new or not used to our style of children's ministry, stay in the background and try to get adjusted to this very different aspect of our children's church. It doesn't take long for most of them to assimilate to the excitement of *Kidz-Turn* in The Castle.

Chapter Five

> ## Side Note
>
> We are located in a major metropolitan area, with families driving from many miles away every Sunday. The fact that we are all hoping to spend eternity together when the Lord returns keeps us motivated, and yet we learned a very long time ago that most of our children do not know each other very well. The thought of spending eternity with folks we don't know can be a little unnerving for some.
>
> So, we begin our services with several fun activities designed to draw children in to participate together, and get to know each other so that they can make "forever friends." You know these activities as "ice breakers." They enable new guests to immediately feel comfortable with their new surroundings.
>
> One of our most popular "ice breaker" games involves a few thousand small Dixie® Cups. Children work together to make various kinds of structures as fast as they can. Some grow to be five feet tall before we call time. You should hear the squeals and screams as their mighty towers come crashing down.
>
> We also have video games that require multiple players and a four-square game. These five-minute, before-service activities are designed for children to make new friends. A good side effect of these "ice breakers" is that our children have already united as a group as the praise music begins.

After the opening video, I step in and welcome everybody. I pray a short prayer, and embed a little tidbit of the subject matter that I cover later in the message. In The Castle, we don't end our prayers with "Amen." Instead, we close our prayers with the words, "It's not about me, it's all about Him," as the children point to heaven.

The next fifteen minutes are in the hands of our praise and worship team. This team consists of children from ages ten to fifteen, and together they form the Knights. Each song is passionately shared to lead The Castle into the Father's presence. If all goes according to our written plan, I step in after the third song, and lead the children in a time of personal prayer that we call "face time with God."

During this time, the children are given the freedom to sit, stand, kneel, and even lay on the carpet to talk with the Lord. I ask them to begin by taking thirty seconds to tell the Lord how much they love Him, without asking for anything from Him. Sometimes, this prayer time can last way more than thirty seconds, and is often more than ten minutes long. As children pray, the Knights play softly in the background and continue to worship.

We have a rule for the Knights that we talk about a lot. They are taught to "play by ear," which means to listen to the Holy Spirit and follow His leading at all times. Sometimes, the Holy Spirit's presence continues so strongly that we do not get into the lesson that I planned. A personal ministry time may occur and supersede it. It is during these prayer times that we see the most growth and the greatest moves of God in the lives of so many of our children.

Now, if everything goes according to our written plan, when prayer time ends, either myself or an appointed child will greet everyone, and recite the rules of The Castle—Sit Tall; Be Quiet; and Participate—followed by the pledge of allegiance, and the pledge to the Christian flag. Then, we take up offering. The offering is placed on a set of old wooden scales in which the boys' scale is up against the girl's.

From here on, I share the message for the day, and follow with prayer, and often more personal ministry. At the close, we have each child return to their seats and await their parents who are more often than not already waiting outside. As The Castle empties out from the first service, the children begin to arrive for the second service, and it all starts over again.

It is important to tell you that even though every service on a given day follows the same schedule and lesson, I have never yet had a repeat service during any of the multiple services on a given Sunday. I believe this is due to the fact that each child is different, and they come with varied attitudes, problems, backgrounds, and levels of spiritual knowledge and commitment. Because of this, sometimes we flip the service,

Chapter Five

beginning with the lesson, and ending with praise and worship. These transpositions are extra special and produce amazing results. When they occur, parents arrive at the end of our service only to find their little ones completely engrossed in the presence of the Holy Spirit, having their young lives being changed and impacted. I could write another book filled with so many exciting testimonies of God's power to change young lives.

Our Sundays are long and often exhausting, but always worthy of praise and filled with blessings. Our young Knights work faithfully each Sunday, and I have never had anyone complain about the multiple services, nor about the effort it takes to pull them off every week. Yes, they get tired and hungry, so we give them some time to unwind between services. We also have a snack area filled with fun items to eat and drink.

As a children's pastor, I have a simple rule that I have kept for decades. I never sit down while there are children present, lest I be swamped with children clamoring to sit next to me or on me. Consequently, as Nancy and I leave on Sunday afternoons, we are both hyped up on a spiritual high, and also completely physically exhausted. We look for the nearest quiet place to rest, eat, and unwind. We take time to analyze and regroup as the exciting plans for our next Sunday begin to turn in our hearts.

Outcomes from The Castle Lessons

As I mentioned before, it would require a second book to give the testimonies of how God changes young lives in The Castle. I would like to share only a few so that you can clearly understand how God moves in our children's church.

One Wednesday night, a precocious, seven-year-old red-head, Charlie Kate, came bounding into The Castle. She almost knocked me over as she screamed, "Pastor Ray! Pastor Ray! We have to pray for people tonight!"

I immediately assured her that we would.

She countered, "But I mean *really pray*, so that God can do what He always does!"

Later, following our worship set, we had the opportunity to pray for several children who had raised their hands. In a flash of red, Charlie Kate prayed down God's blessing on one of these children. The joy; the excitement; the very presence of God's purpose and love poured out of her as she gently placed her hands on the forehead of this child in need of God's help. Charlie Kate knew she was supposed to pray for someone that night, and she came loaded with God's love, just waiting for the right opportunity. For certain, this became memory that would stay in her heart for the rest of her life.

After another amazing Wednesday night service in The Castle, I noticed an eight-year-old boy patiently waiting for me to conclude my conversation with a parent. When I turned to him he replied, "Pastor Ray, how come you know so much about God?"

I could have answered, "Because I study a lot." But instead I wanted to make a very lasting impression on his hungry heart, so I simply and honestly said, "Because I know Him personally, and I have several meetings with Him every day."

The look on his face was priceless as he began to imagine a meeting with God, our Heavenly Father. He would not ever see praying to God and talking with Jesus in the same light again. It is my prayer that from here on he would also have daily meetings with his Heavenly Father.

Deuteronomy 6:5-9 (GW) tells us to:

> [5] Love the Lord your God with all your heart, with all your soul, and with all your strength.
> [6] Take to heart these words that I give you today.

Chapter Five

> ⁷ Repeat them to your children. Talk about them when you're at home or away, when you lie down or get up. ⁸ Write them down, and tie them around your wrist, and wear them as headbands as a reminder. ⁹ Write them on the door frames of your houses and on your gates.

So, how many times a day are you meeting with your Heavenly Father?

As mentioned previously, the Knights are a special group of children, who have grown *so much* in their walk with God that they are called to lead other children in their walks with God. Once a Knight reaches the age when they graduate to an older Sunday service experience, they can choose to become a Knight Mentor. For some children, this responsibility can become a very difficult decision to make.

The upcoming testimony was written by Olivia Jones, who is an incredible Knight Mentor. Before she made the decision to become a Knight Mentor, Olivia served in our children's ministry as a Knight for more than four years. On January 8, 2017, Olivia stepped down as a Knight and chose to become a Knight Mentor, where she will help raise and train the next generation of worshipers. As one of our Knight Mentors tells it, "Our ceiling should be their floor."

Testimony of Olivia Jones
My Last Day, January 9, 2017

Yesterday, (January 8th) was my last day as a Knight of God. It didn't really hit me until that morning, as I handed over my place to a much younger Knight, that I was leaving the KOG. I had been a Knight for more than four years. One has to put forth so much hard work and dedication to be a part of such a special group. I rose through the ranks, first as a Knight

(**Left**) Olivia Jones serving as a Knight Mentor at the knighting of Charlotte Macintosh. (**Right**) Iyanna Jackson's knighting.

Emerging and then on to becoming a Knight K2. One year later, I was blessed to become a Knight of God (KOG). These four years were some of the best years of my life. The Knights of God and the StrikeForce team [an elite group within the KOG] are my family. I wouldn't trade them for the world. Without this spirit-filled group, I wouldn't have the relationship I have with God today. This group has given me so many wonderful opportunities to minister all around the state, country, and internationally. And, I found my calling within these years. That right there says a lot about The KOG team. This KOG team (and every team member) has my heart.

During the summer of 2016, God told me that I will be in a growing season. He told me that there would be good parts but a lot of growing pains. Making the decision to become a Knight Mentor was one of my growing pains. It was so hard to make this decision. I prayed and sought God with all my heart. I was afraid that I would mess up His plan for my life if I made this decision on my own without conformation. Through those weeks of prayer, God gave me this scripture verse:

Chapter Five

> In their hearts humans plan their course,
>   but the Lord establishes their steps
> (Prov 16:9 NIV).

This next step that God is taking me into is Knight Mentorship, active mentorship. Sometimes we have to let go of the things we love, so that God can take us deeper into His plan and our calling. We have to sacrifice to show God we are ready for His next step. It's been a bittersweet time for me but I know it's not goodbye forever. I'll still be with the Knights and my "little Castle babies" that I love dearly but just in a different way. Thank you Pastors Ray Baldwin and Nancy Baldwin for your time and dedication and guiding me into the righteous path of God. I love you! And I can't wait to be trained in leadership with you guys. Also, thank you Eli Mendez Carranza for all your hard work in training us musically and Will Macintosh for your hard work at the soundboard and your wise words during practice! I love The Knights of God team and StrikeForce team so much. Thank you.

—**Olivia Jones**
KOG Graduate & Knight Mentor

Rachel Van Lehr's knighting.

I would like to share another glimpse inside The Castle before we move on to Chapter Six, and specifically describe how "God is on the Move" in our children's ministry. I want to share the perspective of The Castle from another child in our children's church for you to view through her lens, in her own words.

Testimony of Rachel Van Lear

Do I have a testimony? Well, I guess we will be discovering that together in this hopefully, two-paged text. (Oh Lord, help me not to mess this up.) I guess it starts at the beginning of my walk with Christ. That is, if you count it as a walk. It was more like Him calling for me, with an awesome gift, and me just sitting there staring at Him, wondering who that dude was.

You see, when I was a younger kid I just went to church because my parents brought me. My Sunday school consisted of doing craft activity and hearing a Bible lesson. Now granted, we learned many useful lessons and the crafts were fun, but most of the time I was too distracted by the sparkly glitter on the crafts to notice the scripture verses engraved on them. I used to think of church as just a warm up for Sunday lunch. (That is just so sad!!!)

Don't get me wrong. It was good to get me familiar with the scripture verses, but I wasn't truly interacting with them. I remember the only thing that made me curious about this Jesus guy was how others acted during worship. Thank goodness my children's church had worship time! I remember back then it consisted of the children's pastor singing with her guitar in hand. That part of church made me think: "Why were these adults and other kids so excited to sing?" I remember watching their whole demeanor change whenever it was worship time. It was like I was standing outside looking in, watching a display

Chapter Five

of passion and love towards a God I didn't know. That desire to know what this was all about led me to imitate those around me. Of course, at first, my silly younger self just stood in the back acting like I was too cool for this stuff. But, after a while I started to wonder, was I really missing out on something here? So, I started to inch closer and closer to the front during each service, hoping not to draw to much attention to myself.

And just as I was getting comfortable with this new praise thing, my family moved. That led us to a huge church in Texas. Now, I'm not going to name names, but that megachurch did not have a children's church that I liked at all. Worship time consisted of us practicing dances to praise songs, so they could record us for the church's online services. But that did not set my curiosity back—I still wanted to know more about Jesus. In fact, it fueled my thirst for figuring out how to foster a legitimate relationship with Jesus.

After many hours spent on the internet researching new churches in our area, my parents finally stumbled upon *Turning*Point Church. I remember that first time walking into *Kidz-Turn* (The Castle)—I was so nervous. It was a Wednesday night and I did not want to be separated from my parents. But, I remember this random girl greeted me at the door and showed me around The Castle. (I learned her name, Sala, and she became a dear friend).

At first, I thought it was weird that a fellow kid was part of the children's ministry team. But, eventually I came to enjoy having people closer to my own age helping at the children's church. I was so surprised to find out, when Sunday rolled around, that The Castle had a worship band that wasn't adults! They were mostly teenagers, but there were some kids my age at the front singing and playing the guitar. I felt less intimidated and more comfortable coming to the front during praise and worship time because of them. This caused me to truly start to experience what it meant to worship Jesus. I started to actually build a relationship with Him. It was so exciting. I thought I had reached the height of my goal to have a true relationship with God, but boy was I wrong.

It was on a particular Sunday (which I will never forget) that I was enjoying God's presence as worship time was coming to a close. Then, out of the blue, Pastor Ray asked me if I wanted to join the Knights of God . I said "yes" because I didn't know what else to say. I didn't even play any instruments, so I didn't think I could join, but man, am I glad I said "Yes!" Little did I know that my walk with Christ was about to be taken to a new level!

That program has fostered inside me a new understanding of what it means to be a Christian. I learned that to become a leader of change in this broken world, you must first be a servant. Our jobs as Christians are to show everyone the love of God in order to lead them to Christ. Throughout all the mission trips, fundraisers, and worship services with the Knights, I think one of the most important things I learned is this concept of servant leadership.

But that isn't the only thing that I learned as I went through the KOG program. I have always been a shy person. Socializing with people I didn't know was a major anxiety-ridden stressor for me. But, with all the practice and support that my fellow Knights and our leaders offered, I was able to overcome my fears. Heck, these experiences early in my life were the only way that I was able to get through my high school graduation speech! Through all the challenges and triumphs we went through, we slowly became a family. We encouraged each other then and they still encourage me now in college.

Through working in the children's ministry and going on mission trips with the Knights, I also learned humility. In these situations, I always set out to teach others about Jesus and help others with their needs. I thought that it was a one-

Chapter Five

way street—we just give to *them* our time and efforts. What I didn't realize is that they were *teaching me*. I learned so many lessons from those unintentional teachers I was "serving". I learned not to judge people based on their appearances, to savor God's creations, and that sometimes you have to sit back and let God take control of situations.

In addition, being in the Knights not only provided the support system I needed in college, but also the lessons necessary to protect my relationship with God from the temptations and challenges that come with moving away from your parents and your home church. And, that's just the beginning! I can't wait to see how I can use the skills and wisdom I have gained through the Knight's program to continue to strengthen my personal walk with God and to serve Him for the betterment of society.

— **Rachel Van Lear**
KOG Graduate

BEGIN THE CHANGE NOW

If you are a children's minister, remember that it is often easier for children to learn how to praise their Father, and freely experience His presence by singing songs that are considered "kid friendly." Such songs have few words, are repetitive, easy and fun to sing, and have a rhythm that encourages movement. These songs also have mature music and messages that even adults can enjoy. The following are a list of some of our favorites:

- "Alleluia";

- "Here As In Heaven";
- "Come Holy Spirit";
- "Oceans;"
- "Go, Happy Day";
- "How He Loves";
- "Deep Cries Out";
- "Set A Fire";
- "Light Of The World";
- "Come Away";
- "Waiting Here For You";
- "Every Move I Make";
- and "What A Beautiful Name."

These are just a few of our favorites to help you begin. We know you will add others that speak to your children as your ministry grows.

If you are a parent, it is important to know that your child(ren) are hungry for God and spiritual things. You might not know this but they crave knowledge about God and the supernatural. They yearn to have real experiences with their Heavenly Father. They want a deep relationship with Jesus. Please make time every day to talk with your child(ren) about Him and His Word.

In your daily meetings with God, ask Him to give you wisdom and opportunities to share His Word in unique ways with your child(ren). Also, whenever you see that look on your child(ren)'s faces where you know that they have learned something new about their Heavenly Father, stop what you are doing, and enjoy their heartfelt description of what they just discovered. This way, you will always be a part of your child(ren)'s spiritual growth; and what a joy you will have!

In addition, whenever your child(ren) needs to make a tough decision, and they come to you for advice, pray with them. Their faith is "childlike" and very strong. Expect God

Chapter Five

to move as you encourage them to seek God with all their hearts for guidance. Teach them how to do this. Explain how you seek God's guidance. Give examples of several blessings in your life that have arisen from God's grace and your obedience to His guidance.

Also, be aware of times when your child(ren) struggle with letting go of things they love or express fear of change. Share that change can create a deeper relationship with the Lord, and that it can increase their abilities to serve Him. Discuss a time in your life when you overcame a fear of change, how you did so, and the result.

We are witnessing a major move of God's presence in almost every service in The Castle. Children minister to children through prayer and intercession, and experience the love of God in such a powerful way as they simply stand, kneel, or lie down while crying out before God.

Chapter Six

GOD IS ON THE MOVE

"God is on the move!" This was said by a child in The Castle during a service where children were being exposed to the presence of God like never before. At TPC, we recognize the importance of taking the message of Jesus to the next generation. I once read that 83 percent of new Christians are between the ages of four to fourteen.[12] It's time to change and reach out to this worldwide harvest. I personally see it as the single most important endeavor for Christians in the Kingdom of God today.

That being said, I also believe Christianity is one generation away from total annihilation if we don't effectively communicate the Gospel to our children. I know, I'm a children's pastor. I'm supposed to say stuff like that, but I believe it with all my being.

As children's pastors, Nancy and I constantly prepare our children for the greatest move of God since Pentecost! I feel it in my spirit. We have worked with children most of our ministry lives, which is almost one hundred years of combined service. We have never felt the urgency nor the importance of being prepared for this incredible revival event as we do now.

Over the last few years, there have been several prophetic voices declaring that a major move of God is brewing, and it's going to be ushered in through the children and youth. This phenomenon will not be like any past revivals, or moves of God, where thousands were drawn to churches like Brownsville, Toronto, etc. This move of the Spirit of God will happen in local churches where children are being taught about the love of God, and receive the infilling of His Spirit.

In one of her online blogs, Becky Fischer, an internationally known children's minister, describes what this revival will look like: "It will live in the hearts of individual radical, sold out, passionate, little worshipers who cannot be stopped! [These little Christians will be] impervious to doctrinal trivialities, indifferent to denominational debate and polarization, showmanship, cultural pressures, and man-pleasing."[13]

I know this prophesy to be true, because it is already happening at TPC. Tiny voices are being raised to God in every children's service—children who literally can't be stopped as they strive to delve deeper and deeper in their relationship with God. We are witnessing a major move of God's presence in almost every service in The Castle. Children minister to children through prayer and intercession, and experience the love of God in such a powerful way as they simply stand, kneel, or lie down while crying out before God. These defining moments in their lives are so intense that nothing short of entering into the throne room of God will satisfy their deep longing for more of Him.

Our children, who have completely given themselves over to the Spirit of God, go home, and take their parents by surprise. One parent commented as he picked up his eight-year-old daughter, who had been laying on the

Jazzlynn enjoying God's presence.

Chapter Six

carpet for most of the service in prayer. "Honey, are you okay? You are glowing," he spoke in amazement.

With a huge smile, she replied, *"I have been with Jesus."*

The move of God that takes place in The Castle is *awesome* to see. It is a righteous anointing on the children and youth. There is a such level of devotion to the Lord, the likes of which I have never seen before. It has offended some who did not agree with such a powerful anointing, because the anointing centered in the lives of *young* believers.

It has also brought ridicule from some children as these services unfolded. These are the children on the fringes of our services. They are making fun of those involved, and yet when they see God move, it even causes awe and wonder in their hearts. Many adults who have been with us during these services have shared how they felt so privileged to have witnessed the miraculous presence of God's Holy Spirit alive and moving in our young believers.

This revival will not die out after a season because it is not built on a single man. Rather, it will continue to build generation upon generation, until it ushers in the outpouring spoken by the prophet Joel during the last days.

> [28] And afterward,
>   I will pour out my Spirit on all people.
> Your sons and daughters will prophesy;
>   your old men will dream dreams,
>   your young men will see visions.
> [29] Even on my servants, both men and women,
>   I will pour out my Spirit in those days
> (Joel 2:28-29 NIV).

We need to do whatever it takes to expose our children to the presence of God both at home and at church. Become the children's pastor who leads your children in this incredible movement of God. Let the Holy Spirit do His work both in you and in your children. Do not quench this opportunity to see God move, and change not only the spiritual face of your children's ministry but also the world around you. Make your ministry a place where children *find* God.

There will be some who do not initially understand this truth. For instance, several years ago a father told me that he did not agree with the practices of children's church because it keeps the children from seeing their parents worship God. He went on to ask, "Don't children need to be with their parents in order to learn how to act in the church?"

He also believed that what the senior pastor had to teach was important for his children to hear. He went on to state that he believed that the practice of having a children's church was only a simple way of getting children out of the adult sanctuary so that parents could concentrate on worshiping and receiving the Word, unhindered by the needs of their children.

The next week, he pulled his two girls from children's church. They sat in the adult service bored, constantly irritating mom and dad. This continued until their parents had to get them stuff to do to keep them occupied just so mom and dad could have the opportunity to "worship" and concentrate on the Word.

Even in Jesus's day there were adults who felt the same way as this particular father did. The disciples tried to make the children stop crowding Jesus. Couldn't the children see that Jesus was busy talking to adults? When Jesus saw this dissension, he became quite annoyed. He told the disciples to stop what they were doing and allow the children to come to him because, in His words:

> ... for the kingdom of heaven belongs to such as these (Matt 19:14 NIV).

Chapter Six

Is it any wonder why kids hate church? To answer this question, let me ask you one. Do you think that every adult is listening, and being changed by every word you speak? I know that we have to preach with the belief that every heart is being touched, yet as we look over a congregation, we clearly see those who are engaged and those who are not. I love my senior pastor. He is a Spirit-filled, anointed man of God, who can preach, teach, and reach a vast audience who are both saved and unsaved, with incredible results. However, I have yet to find a pastor who has the ability to grab and hold the attention of toddlers, teens, and adults at the same time. Not everyone sees, hears, or understands at the same pace.

Let me give you another analogy. Do you sit a baby at the dinner table, and hand it a steak knife and a T-bone, so that they can eat what the adults eat? Absolutely not.

Do you remember when you were little and *had* to go to church with your mom and dad? Fidgeting, making noises, and thumps on the head. Coloring books and plastic toys used to pacify children. Today, it's iPods, iPads, and iPhones that keep kids busy while they attend church and "watch" mom and dad worship. These days, even teens are predisposed with electronic devices during the adult service. They often don't join praise and worship, or listen to the message. Why is this?

Simple, *it is not their service!*

In my experience, most adult services are not designed nor are appropriate places to reach the children in the church. Next time you have a service, and there are children and youth attending, make a note to see if they are involved during praise and worship, and if they are actually paying attention when the pastor speaks. Many children and teens today are plugged into their devices with ear buds. Often, to hide the obvious wires, they wear their hoodies the whole time.

Also, make a note of how many times parents get up during the service to "take care of" their children. This is a constant problem for many pastors, who while preaching, watch their congregation move and shift, as moms and/or dads with unruly children—or children who need to use the bathroom—get up and disturb others on their way out of their seats. (Why is it that most children end up in the middle of the row or on the front row of a church service?)

Have you also noticed that when an altar call is given, parents tend to either pick up their children, now having a reason not to come to the altar, or they will pick them up and begin to leave? The same thing happens when the offering basket is being passed.

You ask, "Don't children need to learn how to act in church, learn how to praise, how to worship, how to hear and understand the Word of God from the pulpit?"

The answer is a resounding *yes*! Children need to learn all of these things, but this can be accomplished more effectively in rooms solely designed for them in mind, in a place that grips their imagination, and spurs them on to desire being in the presence of God; not in a large, overcrowded sanctuary where everyone towers over them, where they can't see, and get in trouble for standing on the chairs, or bouncing around to get a glimpse of the service. Neither is it to be learned in a cold, beige Sunday school room with hard folding chairs and a reluctant or worn-out teacher using outdated curricula. They need to learn in a children's sanctuary, a themed room they can call their own, filled with color, carpet, and care, and with a children's pastor they can trust and learn from; a church *for* children.

I had a vision many years ago, where I saw the most amazing sight. It was filled

A child spending "face time" with God."

Chapter Six

with children who joyfully entered into what they called their own place of worship. It was designed for and led by children, and watched over by adults. The words "for kids, by kids, and to kids" rang in my head for months. Then, after much prayer and searching, the Holy Spirit poured out the directions of how to accomplish this vision. Today, we have just that: *Kidz-Turn* in the Castle. It is designed for children, filled with children, led by children, and drenched in the Holy Spirit every service.

A typical children's church service at *Kidz-Turn* in The Castle.

Our children learn how to act in church, and how to sit quietly while listening to the exciting truths from the Bible, which are skillfully served in "kid-sized" portions, where they receive just the right amount of truth on which they can act. In The Castle, they learn to praise and worship as they enter into the throne room with songs that they can understand, and to which they can relate. They enjoy what we call "face time with God." They sing, dance, and throw their hands up in adoration, while many kneel or simply lay on the carpet. During times of worship, you can hear a pin drop as children revere the glory of God, the Father, with tears and smiles.

As they grow, they become full-fledged, Holy Spirit-filled children of God—not "little Christians"—with all the power and attributes of any adult believer, and, in many cases, more.

I like something I heard a while back: "There is no junior Jesus or junior Holy Spirit." Children receive the whole experience of God in kid-sized portions and run with it.

Kids are people too. They need an opportunity to meet God on their level. Given the right opportunity they will seek after him wholeheartedly with more fervency than any adult. They need to hear the Word in a way that they can truly understand and to which they can easily relate. They need to hear it in a way that touches their hearts so that they can respond

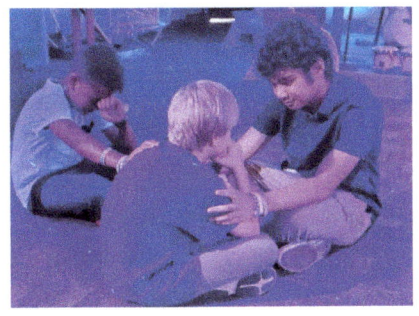

Gian sharing the Word in words they can understand.

appropriately. They need an opportunity to seek God's face in a place where no one cares if they dance, jump, squirm, laugh, sing, shout, and make a lot of noise.

Many years ago, in our very first children's church, we saw God move through children. For instance, one very energetic child, named Kyle, had been touched by the Lord in an amazing way. He loved to dance during praise and worship. However, he wasn't exactly the best dancer; he moved stiffly and clumsily while trying to express himself in the Spirit. During a family service, where adults and children worshiped together, Kyle sat on the front row with his grandparents, while both his mom and dad helped led worship from the platform.

Halfway through the first praise song, Kyle dropped everything, and began to dance. Every time I saw him express his heart for the Lord this way, I am reminded of King David in 2 Samuel 6:21-22 (NIV), when he said:

> It was before the Lord ... I will celebrate before the Lord. [22] I will become even more undignified than this, and I will be humiliated in my own eyes. ...

Kyle didn't care how he looked. He was totally lost in worship. However, this was not "his service." His grandmother quickly reined him in, and sat him down. Next, with a stern look on

Chapter Six

her face, mom asked Kyle what he was thinking, prancing around like a crazy person.

He simply replied, *"I was dancing for Jesus!"*

Children need a place where they can simply kneel on the carpet, lie completely flat on their face, or dance "like a crazy person, undignified" before the Lord—if they want to. They need a place where they can cry out to God without mom, dad, or any other adults getting concerned about them throwing a tantrum, or if they have a problem, trying to step in and *"fix"* it for them. They need a place where God, through the power of the Holy Spirit, can shake them, move them, touch them, fill them, and speak through them without the constraints of what folks think a "normal kid" activity is.

Do you remember when you were a kid? Did you like to climb trees, wade through puddles, play in the mud, kick piles of fallen leaves, run, skip, spin around, and/or dance? Bet you did. Now that you are older, do you still do that?

No? Why?

"Because I am an adult and have grown out of those childish ways"; just as the Bible says you would:

> ... when I became a man, I put away childish things (1 Cor 13:11 NKJV).

Ah, but the Bible also says that if you want to enter into the Kingdom of heaven then you must do so as a little child:

> ... "unless you change and become like little children, you will never enter the kingdom of heaven" (Matt 18:3 BSB).

> "Whoever humbles himself like this child is the greatest in the kingdom of heaven" (Matt 18:4 ESV).

There is a place for doing childlike things. Go out and try it. I guarantee you will love it, and you will laugh as you do it!

The Castle is also a place where we have seen some awesome things happen in the lives of children. *God is on the move!*

"Pastor Ray, this is my first time in The Castle, and I wanted to say, thank you. I have never felt the presence of God before like I did today." Have you ever had a child say this to you? These were the words of an eleven-year-old girl, who with tears in her eyes, then asked, "Is it okay if I come back next week?"

If you could see what happens as the Knights lead us in worship, you would be amazed. Children stand, kneel, and some lie face down. They raise their hands high to God with their eyes closed. Some have tears streaming down their cheeks. You can hear the tiny voices of prayer being lifted up to heaven. I know I keep saying this, reiterating it over and over, but these experiences happen every service, and it's worth repeating again and again.

Some children, who in the past have been hard or difficult to work with, are now moved to a place of worship. For example, I remember a twelve-year-old, who always stood in the back, watching—sometimes not paying any attention—being moved to her knees, head touching the floor, as God moved in and changed her heart. This young girl stayed that way almost the whole service. I studied her when she came back the next week. Instead of standing in the back, she moved up to the front, in anticipation of what God, her Father, was about to do. She wanted to experience true worship again.

Even the adults are moved by God's impressive presence. I heard a visiting parent comment one day that she didn't know that children could pray for each other, lead each other in worship, and minister to each other without an adult leading or stepping in to help them.

Chapter Six

These days, Nancy and I seem to be more like facilitators—individuals who are there to help when absolutely needed. As we stand back and observe what God is doing, we too are moved into true worship.

There is a place of worship and life changing experiences designed to lead children to the Father. There is a place where children can also experience "God on the move" in a way that only a child can. (Oh, by the way, even adults who enter this place also experience "God on the move" the same way.) This place is children's church, and in our church, it's called *Kidz-Turn* in The Castle!

Testimony by Sala Jewel
Giants in the Making: My Experience with
Kidz-Turn and the KOG Program

I remember very clearly going to *Kidz-Turn* for the first time in 2008. If little seven-year-old Sala could have seen how much it would change her life, she would not have complained that the last church was better. It had arcade games. Fortunately, my parents did not listen to my very trivial complaint and we returned the following week. It has been ten years since that first visit and my experiences have truly shaped who I am as a person. I wouldn't trade them for anything in the world.

My brother and his best friends started the Knights of God worship team so, as a young child, I wanted to be a Knight very badly. I told Pastor Ray. He said I would be a Knight-in-Training or a Knight Emerging, creating the first branch underneath the Knights. Working towards my Knighting goal caused me to learn *how to be in ministry.* I learned this around the age of nine or ten. My life revolved around church and school especially since my mom happened to work at TPC (*Turning*Point Church). I was there so much that Pastor Ray and Miss Nancy became family to me. When my dad was gone in another state for work, Pastor Ray stepped in and became a father figure to my brother and me, for which I am eternally grateful. It was kind of funny when people thought I was his daughter or granddaughter. As I grew older and the first generation of Knights moved on, I was Knighted. I became the leader of this second generation of Knights. That is the season of my life where I learned how to be a leader, struggled with depression, and went to England. All of these events taught me so much more about what it means to be in ministry and really helped me begin to come into my own. I stepped out of my brother and sister's shadow. Now, some of my closest friends are from the Knights. My brother even married Brittany, who was a Knight. In summary, since a young age, my personal life has been strongly influenced by the KOG program. Without it, I am not sure where I would be today.

When it comes to ministry, the Knights were what really trained me to have the understanding and skill sets I have now. My mom told me once "Sala, you have to serve before you can lead" so that's what I did. I would help Pastor Ray in whatever way I could. I was like a little personal assistant that was paid in candy. I was determined to be a Knight of God and one day lead it, so I served and rose through the ranks. Through that process, I gained a servant's heart. My growth process soon became less about being the leader of the Knights and more about serving the Lord. Being in ministry is not about being celebrated by man as the great leader of some megachurch. It's about making sure that the Lord gets the glory as you follow the calling He has in your life. The KOG program also taught me how to deal with drama that happens within a team, how to calmly handle disgruntled parents, how to treat sensitive situations (i.e. child abuse), and how to be a leader. I am now on three different adult worship teams. I apply the lessons I learned in the Knights of God all the time.

Pastor Ray, Miss Nancy, and the Knights program

encouraged me in my giftings and guided me in my relationship with God. I remember a conversation with Pastor Ray when he told me it was okay that I spoke in tongues. He taught me that I shouldn't be afraid of it. There are so many other moments like this that I couldn't possibly list them all. Pastor Ray and Miss Nancy guided me in my faith. They helped to give me a strong foundation that I continue to build on. Was my time in the Knights perfect? No, I don't think there is a ministry out there that is. But, I learned and experienced so much! I will never forget or regret being a Knight of God.

— **Sala Jewel**
Former KOG & KOG Graduate

BEGIN THE CHANGE NOW

If you are a children's minister, give your children's church a name. Children want to be able to say where they are going for their worship time. Our children, in particular, want to be able to say that they are "going to The Castle"; "going to *Kidz-Turn*," or any the other names of our children's worship services that we have created in the past. You might even select three or four names, and let your children pick the name they want to call "their church service."

You read in Sala Jewel's testimony that she speaks in tongues. Many children will receive this gift. You will probably want to talk with your children about this gift. You may have to answer questions that they will have, like: "What does it mean?" And, "Why don't all children have this gift?"

If you are a parent and your child(ren) attend the adult service with you, take a moment to watch what they do during the worship service. Are they engaged with the praise and worship? Do they listen to what the pastor is saying? Do they understand the message? If you answer *no* to any of these questions, then you might want to reconsider keeping them with you during your service.

Ask your child(ren) what they learned, and how they felt during the adult worship service. Ask them about their faith and relationship with God. Bottom line, they need to have a meaningful, joyful, up-to-date, personal relationship with the Lord. They might not be getting that opportunity in the adult services. Maybe a vibrant children's church is the key to their spiritual needs. If your church doesn't have one, it might be time for you to talk with your church leadership about creating a children's church.

Also, as a parent, do you notice that your child(ren) are developing leadership abilities at your church? Are they becoming leaders gradually by watching how older children lead their worship service? Are they learning gradually, like children in the Knights-in-Training program? If not, could you suggest to your children's minister that he or she begin such a program? You might even volunteer to become an adult advisor for these leaders-in-training.

Chapter Seven

PLEASE SIR, I WANT MORE

Charles Dickens wrote *Oliver Twist*, the story about a nine-year-old resident in a parish workhouse for orphaned boys. Each boy was issued three meals of thin gruel a day, with an onion twice a week, and half a roll on Sundays. After eating this meager meal, Oliver approached Mr. Bumble, a minor parish official, and said, "Please sir, I want more."

After months, possibly years of starvation, Oliver came to the end. He simply asked for more. Not being demanding nor belligerent, his request came from a deep-seated hunger for more. He was no longer afraid of the consequences. He took a stand for what he needed. In doing so, he possibly paved the way for the rest of the workhouse children to receive more.

I read the other day where Moses, after being blessed many times, approached God, the Father, and said, "Please sir, I want more" (Exodus 33:18, author's paraphrase). Even after so many incredible miracles, he wanted more.

Moses witnessed much of what God had done. He saw and heard God in the burning bush. He observed the many plagues, signs, and wonders God brought in Egypt. He watched the miracle of the Red Sea parting and the destruction of Egyptian armies. He was there when God provided fire by night, a cloud by day, and manna and quail for food. Moses witnessed the children of Israel prosper in the desert, where through it all, not even their clothing wore out. He climbed Mount Sinai, personally met with God, and not only saw God's glory, but also received the sacred tablets bearing the Ten Commandments. Even after he had descended from the mountain, his face shone with the glory of God for forty days.

Anyone would think that all of this would have be enough, right? Look at Moses's reply. He wanted to experience the glory of His presence in a deeper way:

> If you are pleased with me, teach me your ways so I may know you and continue to find favor with you. Remember that this nation is your people (Exod 33:13 NIV).

Moses already experienced God's ways and found favor in His sight. The nation of Israel has, and always will be, God's chosen people. What more would it take to convince Moses of this? However, he was not satisfied; he wanted even more!

Unlike Oliver, Moses enjoyed much of God's blessing and presence throughout his life. Oliver never enjoyed the blessing of enough, let alone more than enough, especially to eat. His request for more was met with anger and indifference, leading Oliver to receive absolutely nothing but more heartache. Moses, on the other hand, received his heart's deepest desire, seeing more of God's glory, and so much more.

I often wonder about today's church, and the hunger that is felt throughout each congregation. Hungry people of all ages often don't know they are hungry until

Lauren asks God for more, and knows He will answer.

Chapter Seven

they taste the goodness of God's salvation. What follows is my constant prayer: "Please sir, I want more."

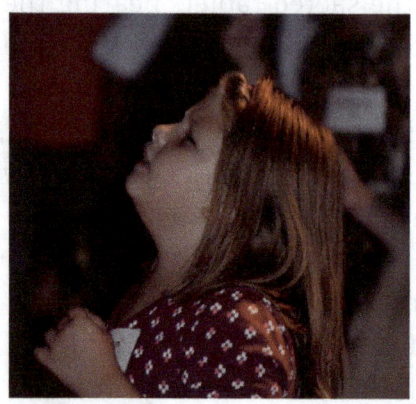

"Heavenly Father, please, I want more!"

Many times, I have sat in cold, indifferent churches without a spark of life and no evidence God's love. Those who attend regularly go in and out, without as much as a taste of what God's menu has for them. Pastors and ministers, who have never seen the bountiful menu that the Lord has made available to them, attempt to feed their flock. It stays this way until the slight scent of the precious aroma coming from the Holy Spirit begins to drift through the sanctuary. Then, the desperately hungry believers begin to cry: "Please sir, there's got to be *more*."

Unlike Mr. Bumble, God, the Father, answers our cries by ladling out from His vast, endless supply, dipping deep into His life-giving bounty. He provides more than enough experiences and substance for all who would cry out for *more*.

In the day just before Jesus walked in the cloudy water of the Jordan, John the Baptist preached repentance. He also shared the good news that there was "more." As Jesus stepped into the water, John said:

> I baptize you with water for repentance, but after me will come One more powerful than I, whose sandals I am not worthy to carry. He will baptize you with the Holy Spirit and with fire (Matt 3:11 BSB).

Jesus came and brought more than repentance. He brought

salvation and everlasting life. Jesus taught that He would leave, however, after His departure, He would send another comforter/advocate to help us. He spoke about the Holy Spirit, of which would bring even "more" to the followers of Christ in the form of baptism by fire and spiritual gifts (John 14:16 GW).

There is Always More!

As I worship in The Castle with so many dedicated young followers of Christ—who have only had a few short years of life to witness God's ways—I am constantly reminded of all the miracles, signs, and wonders that have been my blessings to enjoy. And yet, even I call out for more. I find myself like Moses saying, "That's not enough, I want more" (Exodus 33:18, author's paraphrase). Though, I don't want more as proof of God's love, nor as motivation to carry on; however, I simply want to know Him more intimately and intensely. It is when I ask, that I hear God's voice answer, as did Moses:

> ... My presence will go with you, and I will give you rest (Exod 33:14 NIV).

> ... Ask and you will receive, and your joy will be complete (John 16:24 NIV).

I am eternally thankful there is *always* more for the asking. We cannot risk losing the next generations. Salvation is simply not enough! We need *more* of Jesus, *more* of the Holy Spirit, and *more* of God's amazing power and love! And, our children are starving for *more!* Let's seek God together as we cry out for *more* to take on the most difficult task set before us: we must reach a new generation!

Chapter Seven

The Earbud Generation
The Emotionally Detached & Spiritually Disengaged Generation

One Sunday morning, a young man about eleven years old sat in our children's church. He somehow passed our adult greeters, and mixed in with the group of excited children. He drifted to the corner of the room on the upper level of the bleachers. He did everything he could to look as inconspicuous as possible. His dark, black hoodie almost completely covered his head, totally obscuring his face. He remained still and silent in hope that we would not see him. He even hid his hands and arms inside his huge, hoodie pockets.

When I first noticed him, I kind of wondered whether he was a new guest in The Castle. After a little investigation, it turned out that he had been attending for a period of time. Now, getting that information was like pulling teeth. He absolutely refused to communicate with me. Lacking a name tag, we went out to the registration booth, and got him one, not that he was going to wear it. After several more attempts to communicate, he walked away to the same spot where I first encountered him; hoodie still pulled tight over his head, and emitting no signs of life at all.

My thoughts raced. "What's the story behind this young man? Are his parents here?"

I went out to the computer to check. Yes, they were in the "big kids church", the adult sanctuary. After a while, our praise team cranked up; it was particularly energetic that day. I looked over and still there were no signs of life coming from this boy. His head bowed and his face was covered, he now fidgeted with something in his pocket. This is a fair description of a child, almost all children, in our modern day world. I call them "the Earbud Generation."

Sometimes we think that the "unreached" and "unreachables" are outside the church walls. This is not true. Today, so many of our kids have become unreachable, untouchable, and unteachable. They can be found inside our church walls, hiding in plain sight.

I asked several kids what time they go to bed. Many said 10:00 p.m. on a school night. I thought, "Okay, that might be when they finally hit the pillow." But, I was wrong; that's when they actually end up in their bedrooms. Now, I know kids tend to exaggerate when asked about bedtime, not wanting to look uncool to everyone else, but, the actual time that many of our kids hit the pillow is much later, or should I say earlier in the morning the next day, than we could ever have imagined.

What's going on here? Our kids are like us when we were younger. Remember sneaking a flashlight under the sheets to read a book? Today, kids don't do that. They are on their illuminated devises playing games, Snapchatting, Facebooking, Instagramming, texting, or engaging on some other social media, until their eyes can't focus any more. Their lack of sleep can be seen as they attempt to get up for school or church. If it's not a school or church day, they often sleep till noon or later, only getting up to eat and check if their devise(s) have been recharged. God forbid their charger didn't work while they slept. Pity the parents or siblings who encounter this angry, disappointed, zombie-like, young person searching for a working power source.

I see it during children's church all the time. Children fall asleep, grumpy, uninvolved, fidgeting and totally not listening because they just can't concentrate. Some even come with their devices and try to hide them while no one is looking, as they go right back to what they were doing the night before. This is where I go back to the youngster in the black hoodie we discussed earlier.

Inside his huge, hoodie pocket was his iPhone. He plugged in his ear buds, totally disconnecting from the world around him, and was quite happy to be so. When I asked him to remove them, he pulled his hoodie down, and tried to ignore

Chapter Seven

my request as if I wasn't even there. I finally got an audience with him, and asked why he came church.

"Mom makes me come."

I asked him again to remove the equipment that was pumped noise and images into his mind. Again, he ignored me. I asked if he would rather sit with his mom in adult church to which he replied, "Yes."

As I entered the adult sanctuary to find his mom, I noticed several children of varying ages also sitting with their parents. This was during the worship segment of church in which none of the children stood nor participated. They were totally disengaged with what was going on around them, preferring to engage with the magic of the small device to which they were "plugged into" through earbuds.

Scripture admonishes us to:

> Train up a child in the way he should go, And when he is old, he will not depart from it (Prov 22:6 NKJV).

I particularly like the wording of this verse in the NIV:

> Start children off on the way they should go, and even when they are old they will not turn from it (Prov 22:6).

I cannot imagine what our children will look like when they are older if they are continually enabled to grow up emotionally detached and spirituality disengaged.

Over the years, Nancy and I have said that as parents, teachers, and children's pastors, we hold within our hands the most moldable, pliable resource on the planet, our children. After working in the local school systems for decades, it has become increasingly evident that children are on a potter's wheel being molded. They evolve and their behaviors gradually become worse with each passing grade. Their social skills are almost nonexistent. These turning vessels are somewhat misshapen and almost unusable. Educators rack their brains to find new innovative ways to academically engage this generation of children, amid the unprecedented rise of learning disabilities.

Principal Traylor at Poynter Elementary (Crowley, Texas) explained the situation well when she said, "These days, I have to be a counselor long before I can teach my children."

> **Side note**
>
> This is not the church of tomorrow. These children are the church of *today*. That thought should send chills down your spine.

As Dr. Seuss might say: "What would you do, if this happened to you?"

As parents, what can we do to change this earbud tsunami from stealing the life from our child(ren)? As educators and children's pastors, what are the steps we can take to ensure that not only do we stop this ever growing trend, but that we fulfill our God-given call to reach, teach, and train the next generation?

So where do we start?

Pray! I know you think I say that to every question. (I do!) It is the only logical and sensible answer to a major situation that is brewing and is about to completely boil over throughout our society. It starts with us as parents and leaders.

Television and Video Games are Stationary, Electronic Babysitters

Does this sound familiar? Children, as little as two years old, are mesmerized by a screen, depriving them of all human contact, and creating in their minds a lack of attachment to,

Chapter Seven

or understanding of, real life. I often watch children walk into restaurants with their parents or grandparents for a nice meal, only to sit across the table holding an electronic device, never making conversation with anyone. They only look up long enough to put something into their mouths. I wonder what kind of adults we are creating by allowing this insanity to continue.

Many believe that children who sit in front of the television or begin playing video games at a young age can become addicted to them. They also believe that these behaviors will eventually cause learning difficulties, mental problems, and a lack of social interaction. On the other hand, some believe the opposite. They teach that these activities are advantageous to a child's learning ability. What is a parent to do?

As parents, we need to be involved in everything our children are doing, including watching TV and playing video games. Unfortunately, the age of television has brought many opportunities for parents to use TVs as babysitters. Parents place their children before a screen when they demand too much of their time.

As a child, I didn't have a "telly" until I was about ten years old. My parents called it "the Goggle Box". At that time, there were only two TV stations in England— ITV and the BBC. My family and I were glued to our tiny black and white screen. It was so new that every waking moment was spent with it blaring in the background, with our numerous pairs of eyes watching with every second drifting by. My mom turned it on daily so my younger siblings would have something to do while she worked around the house.

To this day, I struggle with the habit of sitting in front of my 36-inch Vizio as the hours go by, watching other people's exciting lives, or filling my head with the horrors of life. I cannot imagine what my family's life would have been like if we had three hundred plus channels, or video game consoles of every shape and size, flushing mindless garbage into all of our hearts and minds.

I believe there are three things a parent must do to ensure that their child(ren) grow up unimpaired by the technological onslaught that has captured the minds of the younger generations.

First, engage with your child(ren); become involved with their "techie" habits. You don't always have to watch and/or play with them, but you should be aware of what they see or hear. Be aware of what they log into on the internet, and the sites they view. Many sites are unsafe for young minds. They open opportunities for child predators and cyber bullying. Ask your child(ren) often about their online interactions.

Second, set boundaries. Most televisions and cable/satellite services offer parental controls with passwords. Set them high and age appropriately. Make sure your children don't spend hour after hour occupied by the screen.

Third, be a parent. Be inventive. Use initiative to find ways for you and your child(ren) to get away from the electronic interference in your lives. Better still, if you are a new parent, keep your child(ren) from using "personal brain washers" for as long as possible. Many parents don't allow their child(ren) access to electronics, cell phones, etc. For instance, they turn off the TV during meals and family time.

I once had an alarming conversation with a child who complained about their mom spending every minute she could on Facebook, Pinterest, and Amazon music. This child stated that her mom never had time to do housekeeping, cook, or help her with homework. She said, "It's as if I don't exist anymore."

My point is that it is not just children who have become addicted to electronic devices. A new, and more insidious, enemy has invaded and is set on destroying the modern family as we know it. It's time to pray and seek God's face.

As I previously stated, technology can be both advantageous,

Chapter Seven

and quite detrimental to your child(ren)'s development. As pastors, parents, and teachers, it is imperative that we become more deeply educated about the dangers that our children face in order to stem the spiritual encroachment of evil attempting to manipulate and destroy this generation.

We simply cannot stand idly, and watch generations fall by the wayside, as we sing our cute, little action songs. Check out a book written in the mid-eighties, *Devil Take the Youngest*, by Winkie Pratney. This book warns all parents and pastors. I read it many years ago and decided that protecting our children from the attack on their minds should be paramount in my family and ministry.

My God, please help us to understand the severity of enabling our "Earbud Generation" to become emotionally detached and spiritually disengaged.

Testimony of Gian Pedida

Before my brother and I begin, we would like to say that it's such an honor to be a part of writing this book. For the last five to six years, we've had so many amazing children's church experiences that we can't put them all into words in this short space. We are so thrilled to be sharing a few of them with you. We've loved every single moment of this journey and we are looking forward to the moments to come. Now, without further ado. . .

Our names are Carl and Gian Pedida, we're brothers with a one year age difference. [Carl is the oldest, and most of his testimony appears at the end of Chapter Nine.] We are part of the Knights of God in Fort Worth (Texas). We are always self-conscious about the way we refer to ourselves. We are a part of the Knights (of God) is what we prefer to say. A song that I (Carl) used to listen to when I was younger was by Amber Run and it was called *Pilot*. In the lyrics, it says, "I don't want to be the center of anything. Just a part of something bigger." Anytime I would listen to that song, it would simply remind me about how the Knights are put together. The Knights are young people, chosen by God to lead people to salvation and towards a closer and more faithful relationship with our Savior. That has, will, and always will be our standard. Further, if it wasn't for the actions and devotion of every individual in the Knights program, that standard could never be achieved. In our opinion, this concept of unity is our favorite concept in the Knights program. I don't think a lot of people would disagree.

For the two of us brothers, God has blessed us with the gift of music. Playing an abundance of instruments and being able to express these talents means that we are often passed around to different instruments for the worship sets. Because of this, we'll have to admit, it's sometimes difficult to stray away from the notions of the enemy. The curses of arrogance and narcissism can cross the minds of people in our positions. So, it's the most humbling thing to realize that not only are you doing this for the King of Kings and for the people in the room who are seeking Him, but also to realize that it is a joint effort from multiple people who are all working towards the same goal, trying to top our standard.

Although this "unity and being a part of something" is our favorite part of the Knights, we would like to share two other concepts of this program that we believe are just as valuable. We will start with a simple one: the significance of youth.

In December of 2017, I (Gian) was asked to share a short five-minute message in the adult sanctuary about our children's church. I had two weeks to prepare. I had to answer one question, "What does The Castle (our children's ministry) mean to me?" The night I was asked to do this, I went to bed thinking of what to say and also trying to comprehend the situation. I had fourteen days, a prompt, and no idea how to start. As a twelve-year-old, it would've made so much sense

Chapter Seven

to freak out and chicken out. But I didn't have time for that. I had expectations to satisfy (and hopefully exceed) and a lot of research and Bible reading to do. My holiday break from school suddenly became a rush of something more stressful than my school had ever been. After multiple late nights, fifty plus tabs on my computer open, my Bible marked like crazy, and a desperate need for a pillow, I finished a message that was only five minutes long. I know that it sounds insane, but all of the time I spent putting together this message and looking through all the internet articles and Bible passages taught me so much more than I could have ever imagined about myself and the children's ministry that I had been a part of for so long. Two things I learned in particular.

The first thing occurred five weeks after I had given my message. I was visiting the hospital where my mom was recovering from surgery. I was in the seating area by the receptionist desk. I was there for about ten minutes when a lady passed by, and then came back to ask, "Do you go to *Turning*Point Church?"

"Yes, I do," I said smiling.

"Were you the kid who preached that Wednesday night?" she said, starting to grin.

"Oh, yes. That was me." I said, now standing a little bit more upright in my seat.

She got excited, "Oh, I just loved your message. It really blessed me. It gave me a new perspective on kids and the Lord's effect on them. I was really thankful you shared that".

The concept that young people can do amazing things seems like a foreign concept in today's church. So, when kids are seen doing amazing things for the Kingdom, people will more likely than not, be surprised. But that's not necessarily a bad thing. It's that shock that can make today's church pay more attention to children's ministries all over the world. What we need is an upbringing of young people, changing the world, and bringing more of the young generation into the greatness and glory of God.

The second most important thing that I learned was something that I brought up in my message. I was eight when I first joined the Knights. I joined the Knights Emerging, which was basically our program of training for Knights who were starting out. At the time I looked up to this one Knight. (I'm not going to give his name for reasons of my own dignity). I looked up to this Knight on a pretty pathetic and embarrassing level. I followed him wherever he went. I dressed like him, and (bless my little eight-year-old soul) tried to sing like him. One day, this Knight had the opportunity to preach in the Castle. I remember immediately after that service, going to Pastor Ray and asking if I could preach. He gave me a date, and with some help from my parents, I made a pretty simple message on "Obedience Is Better than Sacrifice". I preached the message. I had a few doubts that day, and a few hiccups along the way. But, I got relatively positive and constructive critiques from Pastor Ray, my friends, my parents, and most importantly, the Knight that I looked up to.

That day I realized something. I wanted to preach more often. It was not going to be easy, but I was willing to do whatever it took until preaching became second nature. My parents encouraged me to watch more sermons from different preachers, to get into the Word way more often than I usually did, and to just try to maintain focus.

As I am getting older, this calling to preach the Word of God gets clearer and clearer. I've come to the understanding that the things that I did (and do) in my youth will make or break me.

> Start children off on the way they should go, and even when they are old they will not turn from it (Prov 22:6 NIV).

Chapter Seven

In my five-minute message, I mentioned all of the statistics and scientific explanations for why childhood is the period for growth. The following is an excerpt from the last part of my notes:

> "We can always talk and encourage a young generation to be the ones to change the world for Jesus. After all, Christians have been doing it for centuries now. But in the end, if they aren't taught to be a leader or what it is like to be in God's presence at a young age, then the same pattern will happen over and over. A Silent Generation will be created. I strongly believe that The Castle, along with other Children's Ministries around the world, is organized to break this pattern. Because when you let children wield the power of God, they become unstoppable. It's time for young people to rise up to the calling God has given them. Better now than ever before."
>
> —**Gian Pedida**
> *Current KOG Member*

BEGIN THE CHANGE NOW

If you are a children's minister, you may be intrigued by the program described in Gian testimony. He highlighted some of the standards and components of the KOG Program. One of these components was unity. If you want to learn more about all the components of this program, and how to build a similar program in your church, email Nancy and I at praynan@aol.com for the KOG Manual.

If you are a parent, ask yourself: what you can do to change the "earbud tsunami" from stealing the life from our youngsters? You can save your child(ren) from becoming a member of the "Earbud Generation" by praying, being involved with their technology usage and times of engagement, setting boundaries, and establishing appropriate times to use their earbuds. Redirect your child(ren)'s attention and values away from their dependence upon electronic devices. Help them separate fiction from reality. Create fun activities in which your entire family can participate (e.g., game nights, special trips). Instead of giving electronic gifts, look into the new trends of charity experience-based giving.

What will you begin this week for your family?

Chapter Eight

HOW TO BEGIN A CHILDREN'S MINISTRY, PART ONE

Comments & Questions Heard from Senior Pastors, Children's Workers & Parents

> "Why don't you get a real job, and quit fooling around 'playing church' with a bunch of kids?"
>
> "Children simply can't understand the deep theological meaning of Christ and His church!"
>
> "Children can't get saved; they just mimic what they see in the adults around them."

As you might imagine, these statements are only the tip of the iceberg when it comes to the multitude of questions and comments that Nancy and I have received for more than forty years of ministry. Some of them were very complimentary, bringing much needed encouragement; while others struck deep into our hearts, like fiery darts, seeking to burn and destroy what faith we had left.

After four decades, one statement stuck with us over all the others, voiced by our senior pastor, mentor, and dear friend,

Reverend Dwane Houston, while we were young pastors at our first church in Oelwein, Iowa. Before I share his comment, let me describe the situation we were in at that time.

During the first tumultuous nine months on the job, we survived a tornado that moved our church off its foundation (while we were in it!). Later that same month, a flood swept away the neighborhood where our little church sat. Next, as I stood in the pulpit, I began to faint. Nancy thought I was having a stroke. After an ambulance rushed me to a Cedar Rapids hospital, it was determined that I contracted clinical polio from an Amish family living near a church that we were helping.

Last but not least, the final straw in our ministry there occurred when a young church member threatened to kill Nancy and our young son, Austin. He broke into our home while we were out of town, and left a message in our entry way. It graphically described his intentions. All this happened in our first calling into the ministry, and in less than ten months' time!

Right after these events, as we packed to move to our second church, Reverend Houston took us aside. He relayed one of the most memorable statements concerning our ministry: "God must have something huge planned for you both to have allowed you to pass through these trials over the last few months." It has remained in our hearts since.

We thought about his statement many times, and thanked God repeatedly for the countless blessings that have occurred since. His protection and covering in grace have carried us through many trials and difficulties, including those that occurred after we entered full-time children's ministry.

It would take another book to tell you the countless times the enemy worked hard to derail us from God's plan. Many of these trials came from other pastors and church members. Some came from simply striving to make each day count as

Chapter Eight

we placed one foot in front the other, walking in the belief that God has indeed called us to do something huge.

I am eternally grateful for all that has happened to us. Yes, even the exceptionally difficult times. They have brought the two of us closer together, and, more importantly, strengthened our resolve to serve Christ in our quest to change the world one child at a time. This is the calling God has given us.

We have been asked the following questions repeatedly by many children's pastors and workers, who wish to start or enhance their children's ministries. I hope our answers will guide, and bless your work.

"How Do You Get Your Church Children To Do These Things?"
The First, Easy Answer Is ... Pray

While this is among our most frequent inquiries, it is one of my favorites to answer. I even wrote this book to take time to answer it. Similar questions I constantly hear from children's pastors include:

> How can I get the children involved in my Children's Church?

> What can they do to help in our children's ministry?

The sad thing about most pastors who ask similar questions is that they still think in terms of Sunday school, or keep children engaged in small group settings. They become frustrated because their kids are not getting the message, or they are not interested in anything their church offers them.

Let's answer this question with an example of how disengagement was overcome *one* Sunday. Nancy and I took the Knights to a large church in Colorado, to participate in a summer mission with inner city children. During the two weekends we visited, we were blessed to attend their children's service. The Knights led praise and worship in one of the many designated children's rooms.

Located at one end of this particular room, a large stage with one of the most ornate puppet theaters I had ever seen in a long time, sat there unused, gathering dust. In front of this stage, a much shorter one, about ten feet long by four feet wide, was used by the children's leader to teach his lesson. Huge video screens hovered above him to project preprogrammed segments of the lesson and videotaped versions of praise music, with the hopes that these additions would help the children become interactive.

Our first Sunday there, however, through the leadership of the Knights, the children at this larger church had a totally different experience. At the Knights request, these children stood before the live band, watching peers their own age play instruments and sing live vocals. Many of these Colorado children had never seen a live worship band outside of the main adult worship. They were more than surprised. As a matter of fact, borrowing a word from my English background, the best word to describe the shock we witnessed would be to say that these children were "gobsmacked." Most of the children and adults stood amazed, eyes transfixed, and watched.

I also noticed that even though the songs were familiar and the lyrics were displayed on the video screens, not one mouth moved, and not one voice sang in praise, except for those on stage, the Knights.

During the second song, I saw two more adults walk into the room. They were just as surprised as the rest of the parents present to see a live band in the children's church. Everyone enjoyed the performance; even the adults who led the church's children program were quite moved by the team, and their

Chapter Eight

anointing as they played and sang. Because of the success of this Sunday service, we were invited back the next week.

The second Sunday was even more exciting. Our team literally chomped at the bit to lead the children in worship once time. Though, this time it was very different. A larger audience eagerly awaited our arrival. The atmosphere was charged with expectant anticipation! That day, disengagement ceased—all on one Sunday.

As the Knights began to sing, the Colorado children began to move about, tapping their feet, and even a few hands began to clap. I further surveyed the group and realized that several little voices began to sing along. It was totally awesome. Even our worship team grew more animated than the week before.

Halfway through the worship service, the senior pastor stepped in, making his yearly rounds through the various departments, checking in to see how everything was going. The moment he walked into our service, his eyes fixed upon the stage. Our team was totally involved in leading the children in praise and worship.

I heard him ask, "Are these our kids?"

As he watched in awe, a young teen leader in his church, Charlotte, replied, "No, they are from a church in Fort Worth."

His next question put fuel to a fire that had been lit in this young teen's heart for the rest of her life a question we have heard over and over: "How can we get our kids to do this?"

Charlotte moved to this very large church from TPC over a year earlier. She had been one of our young Knights. She prayed, shared, talked, and waited on the Lord to bring this question and moment to fruition. Since her arrival, she made it her mission to recreate the children's worship experience in her new church that she had at our church. The fire lit that day. You can read her about passion for worship, in her own words in her upcoming testimony. I believe it will bring tears of joy to your heart.

Testimony of Charlotte Macintosh

At the age of seven, my heart was set on being a part of the Knights of God worship team. From the beginning, my entire family was invested in the children's ministry of *Turning*Point Church. I had no idea what opportunities were to come in the course of our five years of participation.

> [3] Children are a heritage
> from the LORD,
> > offspring a reward from him.
> [4] Like arrows in the hands of a warrior
> > are children born in one's youth.
> [5] Blessed is the man
> > whose quiver is full of them.
> They will not be put to shame
> > when they contend with their
> > opponents in court
>
> (Ps 127: 3-5 NIV).

The mission of the KOG is to give children an opportunity for a personal relationship with Christ, with the KOGs working to give children comfort and security in their faith. During my time in children's church, I attended three mission trips in which I worked with different groups and teams around the country. Not only was I given the chance to share the amazing love of Jesus, but I grew immensely in my own relationship with God. And, I learned to stand firm in my faith.

One of the many amazing things about the KOG program is the message it gives. The program places children from the ages of seven to eighteen in leadership positions. Teaching skills and confidence needed in everyday life, the Knights of God allow children to place their eyes on God and be lights in the lives of others. In today's world, there are many negative influences placed in the minds of children. Expectations such as being beautiful, making good grades and excelling in sports can infect our minds with the idea of perfection. The Knights of God gives everyone a safe place to know God, and build relationships with Him and others that last a lifetime.

Pastor Ray knighting Charlotte.

Being given the opportunity to be a part of this amazing group of people and in the lives to both children and adults around the world has truly been a gift. I wouldn't change it for the world.

—**Charlotte Macintosh**
Roving Reporter for KidzNews

Before I answer more of the question—"How do you get your church children to do these things?"—I would like to share some of the many unsuccessful, and unproductive answers I have heard from other children's church leaders/workers over the years. These are *not* answers I would give you. As workers in children's ministry, you *don't* need to get kids involved by training them to do small tasks like:

- handing out snacks;
- picking up the trash;
- taking a younger child to the bathroom;
- playing a tambourine;
- reading the scripture verse for the day; or,
- taking up the offering.

To show how often these attempts have failed, one church was so adamant about "taking up the offering" as the go-to method to get children involved in the worship experience, that they insisted that all offering takers must be over ten and attend a class on responsibility before being allowed to take up the offering. My point is that while these activities can be done by children, they are not the key to getting them involved in their own worship experience. Moreover, I truly feel that we have seriously underestimated the value and abilities of the children God has placed in our hands.

I love the verses in Psalm 127:3-5 (AMP):

> 3 Behold, children are a heritage and gift from the LORD,
> The fruit of the womb a reward.
> 4 Like arrows in the hand of a warrior,
> So are the children of one's youth.
> 5 How blessed [happy and fortunate] is the man whose quiver is filled with them;
> They will not be ashamed
> When they speak with their enemies [in gatherings] at the [city] gate.

God placed children in our hands, yes even the little ones who are often unruly and out of control; children who are endowed with monumental and unlimited abilities, potential, and possibilities. I know you have heard this many times: if arrows (children) are carefully aimed, and well shot from the hand of a skillful archer, they will not only hit the target, but also go farther than the one shooting, aiming and guiding the arrows. My goal in life is to help children go farther, and do more than I ever have. They will reach higher heights and accomplish greater things than I ever will. To achieve this goal, I work hard to train both myself and those under my ministry to strive for the very best in ourselves as we "run the race set before us" (Heb 12:1, author's paraphrase).

Chapter Eight

Jesus himself told his disciples:

> "...[you] will do the works I have been doing, and [you] will do even greater things than these, ..." (John 14:12 NIV).

Jesus shot twelve arrows from his bow, and forever changed the entire future of the world. He also did something else; Jesus didn't just grab the first twelve people he saw, he *personally chose* his twelve. Why do you suppose he did that? Was it because they looked good, had money and influence? Or, maybe they already knew a whole lot about ministry, and God so that it wouldn't take much work to get them ready for their world-changing task?

We know these qualities were not his criteria. If they were, he surely would not have chosen Simon Peter, a simple, rough-and-tumble fisherman. Nor would he have chosen Matthew, a well-known and hated tax collector. Jesus *spiritually profiled* his twelve disciples. Each had unique abilities and talents.

To illustrate my point, let's look at Simon Peter. Why Simon Peter? He was loud and tenacious, a simple man who wouldn't quit. Remember when he fished all night and caught nothing (Luke 5:5)? If I fished for a couple of hours without a bite I'd totally be done. I would pack up and leave the lake with an attitude way too low to want to ever go out again. Yet, Simon Peter went out again and again under the hot sun when he knew from years of experience that there were no fish to be had at that time of day. But he went out because Jesus asked it of him. He was strong and capable; a diamond in the rough!

In our children's ministry, we take our lead from Jesus. We profile our kids! I know it's not politically correct to profile anyone, but we did, and still do. We *spiritually profile* them. Let me explain.

Before you attempt to get your children more involved in

their worship experiences, you first have to ascertain how long you plan to be in this God-called position of reaching, teaching, and training children for the Kingdom. Are you called to do this work for Christ, or are you on the steps to a higher calling? Is children's ministry your final goal in ministry, or is it to become a youth pastor, senior pastor, or some other position? Is your intent to grow a church, or are you simply a flash in the pan?

As I wrote earlier, Nancy and I floundered in our children's ministry due to the fact that we couldn't find a soul (adult) who would be willing to join us in the back room of oblivion, commonly known as the children's department. We always asked our senior pastor for help, begging as it were, for anyone to come help us, but to no avail. It was going to be the two of us and no more.

Then, one particularly difficult day, we prayed in desperation for God to send us someone, anyone, we didn't care who, to help before we totally gave up and quit. Our prayer did not bring us what we so eagerly wanted, but rather, it came with the most unusual answer that totally transformed our hearts and direction.

The Lord simply said: "Train the children!"

How Do You "Train the Children?"

"'Train the children,' really? But Lord, *we* need help with the children."

At this point, we stopped and asked ourselves the same question I previously posed to: how long were we going to be in this? Our answer has always been that we are in this for as long as it takes to change the world one child at a time. Then, God's answer hit us square in the heart; if we trained the children *now* we would always have the ministry *help* we needed in order to complete our calling.

Chapter Eight

Therefore, we began with our first child, our son Austin. He was about three years old at the time. We still laugh about the days when he became our first, life-size puppet. Almost immediately, as Austin started, we saw one little boy, (who previously and constantly tapped his pencil on his desk during our lessons, pick up a small set of bongo drums. As he played, we watched a little girl begin to dance to his music. We instantly realized that she loved dancing, so we began to teach her the motions and steps to accompany several songs. Then, this boy and girl began to help us during our kids' praise and worship, becoming the first of many young worship leaders to step up to the plate!

Again, we spiritually profiled our kids; we saw their natural talents/potential. We used these gifts to enhance our children's ministry. From then on, we began to watch all of our children. Those who were musically inclined, we taught them to play guitars, drums, and keyboards. We also looked for those who enjoyed singing, and taught them to lead their peers in praise and worship. We saw kids who enjoyed using the puppets, and taught them how to become puppeteers.

We looked for the ones who wielded the biggest smiles and had the most outgoing spirits. We gave them official name tags and taught them how to greet other kids. They became our ushers and greeters. The list goes on.

Spiritual profiling has become a major ministry within our children's ministry. We don't just minister to kids; we teach and train them to do the work of the ministry too. Every child is a minister, every child is given a task, and everyone has responsibility. Our children have become our most trusted and capable volunteers. As the years unfolded and the children grew, we retained many of them to become youth and later adult workers/leaders.

Today, every aspect of our worship service is conducted by children. No adults. We *only* have children on the platform leading praise and worship. We *only* have children running the sound and video booth. Furthermore, it's now quite rare for me, as the children's pastor, to actually lay hands on children who ask for prayer. These days we have powerfully-trained children who are the intercessors in our children's church.

One of the most fulfilling blessings of children being involved in their own worship service is to be able to step back, and allow the Holy Spirit to move at the hands of children ministering to children. There is a very special spiritual touch children have when they minister to their peers. They have an uncanny understanding of the needs and feelings of each other. When they intercede for one another, those prayers become supersized in the hearts of those receiving them.

For example, I once watched one of our young intercessors, Eva, pray for a little girl during our Sunday worship service. Eva knelt down in front of this weeping girl, and with a tender voice, asked what she needed. After a moment they hugged each other, crying, both receiving from the Holy Spirit.

As a second illustration, when Gian—whose testimony you read in Chapter Seven—was a vibrant young twelve-year-old, he began praying for a line of children who all waited to hear from God as they brought their needs to the altar. He laid his hands on the first child and after a short, but intense prayer, that child dropped to the floor. The second did the same. As Gian moved down the line, almost all the children had fallen under the power of the Holy Spirit.

Throughout this children's church service, there were children lying all over the carpet. Many others moved from one child to another with everyone praying for each other. This gave rise to several other children who began to sense God's touch on their lives. They too began to pray and intercede for others. The real fun began as adult workers and even parents came forward for prayer. They also ended up doing a little carpet time, being overcome by the Holy Spirit.

Chapter Eight

As a third example, Carl, Gian's brother, while playing the keyboard, sensed the movement of God, and began to play and sing through spirit at fourteen. The few adults who were in the room that day, after overcoming the shock and awe of God's presence moving in this service, began to minister and be ministered to by children.

Services like these are not only common in our ministry, but are very powerful, leaving children and adults with a deeper sense of God's love and grace. They also plant a desire to be used by God among those—children and adults—who are present; a desire to do the work of the ministry.

Charlie Kate was one of these children. She was a recipient and a witness of what the Lord had done in the lives of her friends in children's church because she was one of those who had spent a little "carpet time" during a moment where the Holy Spirit touched her deeply. The next Sunday service, she arrived early, made a beeline for me with a huge smile, and jumped up-and-down as if she would burst.

I get asked this question more and more from children who see and feel the power of the Holy Spirit: "Pastor Ray! Pastor Ray! Are we gonna pray for people again this week?"

I replied that, yes, we would.

"You know, like really pray where God touches everyone?"

"Yes, I'm sure we will," I reiterated.

"Pastor Ray! Pastor Ray! Can I pray for someone too?" There is hardly a week that passes in which new children do not ask to become more involved in our children's ministry.

As stated previously, our children's worship team is called, the Knights of God. These children minister during each of our multiple Sunday and Wednesday services. They work in several other areas of the church as well. One of the greatest blessings we received was when we realized that we have Knights who have graduated and now participate on every worship platform of our church—in the young adults', and adults' ministries.

As they grow up, they also became volunteers, fully trained and vested in their church, reaching out through praise and worship, preaching, interceding, caring for babies and toddlers, as well as teaching adult classes.

In conclusion, don't underestimate the absolute blessings and gifts God has placed in your hands! If we don't teach, train, and lead the children who attend our church while they are young, then we will see the decline of our church in the next generation. The church is always one generation away from total annihilation. *Train the children!*

BEGIN THE CHANGE NOW

If you are a children's minister, train your children by spiritually profiling them. Identify their natural inclinations and abilities, and give every child a responsibility that relates to their gifts and talents. Each child is trained in one or more ministries; each child is a minister. Ensure that you train them on the basics of responsibility. Encourage them to come to you as the year progresses with new ideas on how to improve their areas of responsibilities so they can serve God more completely.

We identified some areas of spiritual profiling that have been successful for us. These are some that we recommend:

    Singers
    Greeters
    Puppeteers
    Worship leaders
    Musicians
    Intercessory prayers
    Media specialists
    Pastors

Chapter Eight

Yes, even pastors; I am constantly on the lookout for my replacement. Right now there are two young people in our Knights program who could easily take over my position, if needed.

We know you will think of other areas of ministry where your children are especially gifted. We recommend that you sit back a few Sundays, and list those whose talents you have not yet profiled, or invite a parent or congregation member to observe the children, so that their fresh perspectives can be added to yours.

If you are a parent, speak to your children's pastor about a special gift(s) your child(ren) possess. Also, offer to bring instruments and media equipment that can assist children in their worship services. If you play an instrument, could you volunteer to teach children in your church's ministry to play that instrument?

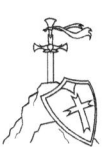

Take a good long look at what you are doing as a children's minister. Ask yourself, "Is what I'm doing really working?"

Chapter Nine

HOW TO BEGIN A CHILDREN'S MINISTRY, PART TWO

Comments & Questions Heard from Senior Pastors, Children's Workers & Parents

Let's continue answering questions you may have about starting your children's ministry.

"Can Children Really Get Saved?" or "Can Children Really Hear from God?"

I once heard a well-known pastor teach how children are not capable of being saved because their minds and spirits cannot grasp the true meaning of salvation. He went on to say that, in fact, whenever you see or hear of children giving their hearts to the Lord, they are simply mimicking what they have seen the adults do around them. His whole idea for children's ministry was to occupy the children while their parents attended the adult service. He continued, "Actually, the children need to be in the adult sanctuary with their parents participating in the praise and worship, and listening to the Word of God."

I wonder how that really works in practice. Let's look at the some famous folks who got saved early in their lives. I know Samuel was given to the Lord after he was weened (1 Samuel 1:24, author's paraphrase). His mother, Hannah, made God a promise that if He would grant her a child, she would dedicate him to the Lord (1 Samuel 1:11, author's paraphrase). So, around the age of three, Samuel was given to Eli, the priest, to be raised in the temple.

According to Josephus, a first century historian, when Samuel was eleven years-old he heard the voice of the Lord speaking to him. After a sleepless night, Samuel received a special word from God. He interrupted Eli's sleep several times. Eli told him the voice he was hearing was God's and, if He calls you again, then you must say:

> "... Speak, LORD, for your servant hears." ...
> (1 Sam 3:9 ESV).

Eli was probably like most adults who are awakened several times in the night. Not expecting the child to know much, he sent Samuel on a wild goose chase—to hear God's voice.

God, on the other hand, expects a lot from children. There are many high expectations for children in the Bible.

So, Samuel returned to his bed, but did not sleep deeply because he knew God was going to talk to him that night.

It's really sad how children are overlooked and pacified in church society today. The church expects so little of them. One of my favorite sayings comes from famous British inventor, Alan Turing, said in a speech during the Second World War:

> Sometimes it is the people no one can imagine anything of who do the things no one can imagine.

Chapter Nine

Let's get back to Samuel. Once Samuel responded, the Lord told him that the wickedness of Eli's sons resulted in their dynasty being condemned to destruction (1 Sam 3:13, author's paraphrase). In the morning, Samuel hesitated to repeat the message to Eli, however, Eli asked him to honestly recount what the Lord had told him (1 Sam 3:15, 17, author's paraphrase). When Eli heard the word that God had given to Samuel—Samuel actually understood what God had told him—Eli merely said that the Lord should do what seemed right (3 Sam 3:18, author's paraphrase).

What is God thinking, giving such strong words to children if they cannot grasp their importance or meaning? Truthfully, not only do children understand but they can have a real, meaningful relationship with the Lord.

There are several more major figures in the Bible who were called" and used by God as children, e.g., Josiah was only eight when he was called. In today's world, Billy Graham was sixteen when he gave his life to God. Billy Sunday was ten years old when he began his incredible journey with the Lord. The cross-carrying, world-trekking evangelist, Arthur Blessett, was seven when his life changed forever. My wife, Nancy, was eight when she responded to the call of God. That day, God told her that she would be the mother to many children. Over the years, the number has climbed into the thousands. The list could go on and on.

I have personally led thousands of children in the prayer of faith. Each one received a new life; some were as young as three. I have watched children line up from one end of the altar to the other in order to receive Christ, not because everyone else was doing it, but because they felt the very presence of God calling them to make a decision to follow Him. I cannot tell you the number of children I have personally baptized, or prayed for to receive the Holy Spirit. I have seen children pray for other children to be saved and healed. I have witnessed numerous children pray with their parents to be saved.

If children cannot understand the deep things of God, why does Jesus tell us in Matthew 18:3 that we need to become as little children to enter the kingdom of God (author's paraphrase)? Do not be misled. Children can, and will be saved. Truthfully, it is easier to lead a child to Christ than it is to lead an adult!

"What Do I Need To Do To Change The Way We Do Things?"

I distinctly remember one time when a children's ministry director asked me, "What do I need to do to change the way we do things?"

She was very discouraged and disappointed with the church. At one time, she dreamed of doing great things for children, but over the years, she had not fulfilled any of her aspirations. I know for a fact that there are many other children's ministers out there who feel the same way.

Take a good long look at what you are doing as a children's minister. Ask yourself, "Is what I'm doing really working?"

It is true that: "If you [continue to] do what you've always done, you'll always get what you've always got[ten]."[14]

Some say that is the art of foolishness. Instead, change the way you do things, and pray earnestly. Seek God's plan, use your God-given imagination, and walk one step at a time in faith as you venture out in search of a better plan for your children's church.

I feel I need to say this before we go any further: as children's ministers, we, in no way, ever need to change the message. What is needed today is a new package; a new way to present the Gospel in a manner that grabs a child's attention and allows their own imagination to explode with excitement.

I first started teaching children in my home church in

Manchester, England, in a small, dingy Sunday school room that was as damp as it was cold. I was miserable but I didn't know any better. Bless those few little ones who continued to come week after week. When Nancy and I moved to the United States to work as student pastors at her home church in Chariton, Iowa, almost immediately we began to teach Sunday school to children in a small classroom in the basement. This class was totally different from the one in England. It was colorful and warm, with nice chairs and a table. We even had pretty pictures on the wall and a small projector. However, this room had one similarity to the one in England. Other than the supply closet, it was the most boring place in the building!

Then, we moved our class upstairs to a larger room, where instead of Sunday school, we held our first children's church. The difference was amazing. The children were excited, engaged, and ready to learn. It was here that we began to seek the Lord about teaching and training the children. Here we saw children rise up and find their place in the Kingdom. We took time to talk with the senior pastor about his vision for the church and for the children. We began to imagine what would grab the children's hearts and imaginations.

"So Where Do I Start?"

Pray Earnestly and Then . . .

To begin, talk to the children and youth in your church. Find out what trips their triggers! If you are moving to a new church to take over the children's department, or even if you have been at your church for a long time, find out the church's and community's histories. Is there something famous or interesting about where you live?

Visit, or send a trusted representative to visit, several children's churches around the town or within driving distance. Check out what they are doing. Most themes are not copyrighted, so if you see something you like, take it home.

For years, we have had scores of churches and children's workers visit our ministry to see what we're doing. What I love the most when they come is talking about what we do. We load them down with everything we have ever written and/or produced. Seeing the adults' faces as they walk into *Kidz-Turn* in The Castle—an actual Castle—for the first time is priceless. You can see the wheels turning faster and faster as they walk around touching everything, including the swords on stage. We enjoy hearing the results, months later, after they returned home and repackaged their message.

Talk with the parents and Sunday school teachers. Ask them questions like:

- How healthy is our children's ministry, or our Sunday school?
- Are our children hearing, learning, and responding to the Gospel?
- Are we retaining the children and youth?
- Are we training new Christian leaders among our children and youth?
- Are we reaching new families?
- Are we relevant?
- Do we have more children and youth attending the adult services than your Sunday school/youth activities? (This is a big one. If your children are not coming to your children's services, find out why and make changes.)
- Are we teaching material or sharing Christ?
- Do our children have a ton of knowledge about God and Jesus, or do they have a vital relationship with their Savior? (It is not enough to simply teach the lesson, we *must* create an atmosphere where children can find Christ, and nurture a relationship with the risen Lord.

Chapter Nine

As one of my young Knights states, "Get down and personal with Jesus.")

I constantly pray over the children having a personal relationship with the Lord. It concerns me more than any other part of my children's ministry. I always ask: "Is our ministry creating the right atmosphere for children to develop a one-on-one, personal relationship with Jesus?" Anything else is just fluff and often unnecessary. Head knowledge is a killer for those who want to know God or can't find a place to get to know Him personally. Heart knowledge is what I want our children receive; a constant, every day, life-giving stream of God's love and blessing.

"How Do I Come Up with a Theme?"

First, pray. Second, pray some more; third, pray and then write it down. As I said earlier, your local and cultural history can be an incredible source of inspiration for themes. Let me give you a list of the themes that we have been involved with over the years:

- a castle
- a railway station
- a hacienda
- a forest (the original SureWord)
- an old western town (SureWord)
- a western town (Buffalo Bill)
- a small town
- a fifties cafe

Notice that "a castle" is listed first. Many people have asked, "Why would you have a castle in Texas?"

I know it sounds a bit out there, but it was the right thing to do. Let me explain.

We first started with an old western town called "SureWord Township" with Marshal Ray and Miss Nancy; Chief Nowannasin of The Friendly Deep Woods Indians; Long Tall Tex (a stilt clown) who acted as mayor; Black Jack Shelack, the notorious villain and his gang, the Chance Boys: Slim Chance and No Chance; J.J. Scuggins, the mountain man; and, the list of characters went on. We eventually built the town in a huge, outdoor circus tent because we had outgrown the building's children's facilities. For eighteen months, we met in the tent, rain or shine, with hundreds of very excited children. After the adults built their new sanctuary, we moved the whole thing back inside into the old adult sanctuary. However, a western theme just didn't seem to be the right fit. So, we prayed and God gave us an amazing idea.

Hailed from England, I have always enjoyed castles, kings, Robin Hood, and tales of the Knights of the Round Table. From there we began to create a whole new cast of characters: Raymond Goode and Lady Nancy; Much, the puppet; Sir Laughsalot; The Sheriff of Naughtyham; Benny and Sally Vation; and, again the list of characters goes on. With the help of Dustan Puckett, a local businessman, we designed and created a seventy-five-foot long castle that was over twenty-feet tall. It had a working portcullis and two, huge puppet stages, lighted rooms, and many other fantastic attributes. Much of this was done at little or no cost.

How? I'm glad you asked.

We began vision casting, sharing this dream and idea with everyone who would stop and listen. A local overhead door company heard about us and asked if they could help install the portcullis, while another local man made the portcullis from steel pipe. Another company came in and did all the drywall for free. We located a Styrofoam company in Mansfield, Texas, who made, and donated the entire castle front, while another local company gave us the stucco finish. We needed a giant double door that hung in an archway leading into the castle, and our good friend, Dustan, designed and made this incredible, giant hobbit-like doorway.

During this time, we concentrated on training the children. Our praise team only included children and young teens. Our children leaders worked many hours gutting and repainting the entry outside The Castle doors. The day we finally opened the doors for the children and parents to see was absolutely momentous. Gasps and shouts could be heard everywhere. We saw unending smiles and even tears of joy as everyone wandered around this awesome new facility. One little boy whose imagination exploded that day, fell to his knees and asked: "Is this ours?"

My answer was *absolutely*!

For years this theme has stood strong, and to this day is still in use, even though Nancy and I have moved on to a new children's ministry. Yes, just in case you were wondering, we built a castle, in this new ministry (TPC), too.

Do You Make It Age Appropriate?

Always! We learned many years ago that age matters and that our age limits are very important. Children learn at many different levels. So we have different, age-appropriate settings.

Overall, at TPC, our children's ministry is called *Kidz-Turn*. We start our grouping with ages five and six, in a "pre-children's church" setting called *Wee-Turn*. Then, for ages seven to twelve, we have *Kidz-Turn* in The Castle. Several have asked if having seven-year olds and twelve-year olds in the same room works, and the answer is absolutely. The twelve-year olds become helpers and often mentors for the younger children. They help keep the younger ones under control, and the younger children tend to look up to the older ones.

During our worship time at the beginning of the service, we invite our younger children from *Wee-Turn* to join us. This is very intentional and an important move. First, it gives us a chance to introduce the younger children to The Castle. Their energy and exuberance is totally infectious, giving way to childlike joy in praise through dance and excitement. Second, it gives us the chance to watch the youngest children, to see which ones are the most engaged and to see the ones who are not. This is when we begin the process of training those who have a deeper tendency toward spiritual things as potential leaders. This is also when we have the opportunity to plant love and pay more attention to those who are not responding to God's love as much as we would like.

We want every child to succeed in church and gain a personal relationship with Christ. Every year, we have some children who don't show any desire to praise or worship because they are either very timid or very hyper. However, through love and nurturing even these most disinclined children become great leaders.

"How Do You Disciple Children?"

This is another most frequently-asked-question in our ministry. You will likely recall how we use puppet people/ fur feathers and friends, StrikeForce and the Knights Program to establish a very successful, well-structured, disciplined program. It has worked so well, that after only ten years at TPC, our Knights assume leadership positions in all ministries of our young adult and adult ministries without any additional training in discipleship or self-management. Our program *really works!*

How do we discipline our children? One child at a time! The following section describes how we do that.

Chapter Nine

What Discipline Rules Do You Follow?

We have three simple rules:

1. **Sit tall**, in total control of yourself.
2. **Be quiet**, listen and show respect for leaders and friends.
3. **Participate**, be engaged in what *Kidz-Turn* is doing whether singing or listening.

What does this look like in practice?

God's Word states in Proverbs 10:17 that discipline is a way to life (author's paraphrase). Therefore, for us discipline is a "teaching moment" not punishment. We want to explain the difference between the two. Discipline is training that corrects, directs, molds, and perfects a person mentally and/or morally. Punishment, on the other hand, is suffering, pain, or loss that serves as a penalty inflicted on a criminal. Hence, when these "teaching moments" arise, we are both understanding and caring. When disciplining a child, it must always be done consistently and in love. We treat each child with the same love and care, noting their special physical, mental or emotional needs. With all of this information in mind, here are the three "redirection steps" we follow when a child is struggling to participate.

First redirection: A worker encourages the child to participate appropriately. Then, that worker places themselves next to, or very close, to the child.

Second redirection: This comes only after the child continues to misbehave. At this point, the child is quietly removed from the room. The worker, along with a second volunteer, takes a moment to chat with the child. The worker asks the child: "Why did you have to come out of *Kidz-Turn*?"

If the child cannot verbalize why, the worker reminds the child of the three rules — sit tall; be quiet; and participate.

Then, the worker asks the child, because we want this to be a teaching moment, "Which rule were you having trouble with?"

The worker explains that we have these three, simple rules because we are a large group and we want to enjoy our time together safely. Then, they pray together and quietly return to *Kidz-Turn*.

Third Redirection: This should be avoided at all costs. It means your opportunity with the child is over. At this point, their parent/guardian is asked to come help and/or the child goes with them. We always explain why this action is necessary and that the child will leave this week's service, but may return to the next week's scheduled class, as long as he or she apologizes and agrees to be the best that he or she can be.

We have taken discipline to a higher level by installing video cameras in our rooms and hallways in order to visually share the problem with the parents. These cameras also protect both children and workers from wrongful accusations.

Let me share one of our favorite discipline stories from over a decade ago. His name was Gabriel; not the angel! He first arrived at The Castle as a seven-year-old, dropped off by what we understood to be his grandmother. He stomped in and sat down with gusto a few feet from one of our regular Castle kids, who happened to be one of the most well-behaved. At the other end of The Castle, Nancy visited with a few of our little girls when she saw Gabriel stand up, clinch his fist, and plow into the little boy next to him. Nancy recalled jumping instantly into action the very moment she saw the clenched fist. But, you know how things like this unfold in your dreams, when everything goes into slow motion; you try to get there before the punch lands, but you just can't move fast enough.

After ascertaining the welfare of the little guy who now displayed the onset of a perfect black eye—imagine explaining that to mom and dad—we separated Gabriel from the ever-growing crowd of witnesses, who all shouted their version

Chapter Nine

of what took place. Nancy and another worker took Gabriel out into the hallway to find out what actually happened. (It is also important to note that we never reprimand a child in front of their peers.)

> **Side note**
>
> Every hallway in our church has security, with video cameras recording at all times. Whenever movement is detected, it is captured. We always take our children, who are in need of assistance, into the hallway, outside The Castle doors where a camera and microphone are located to be sure that everything said and done is recorded on video. I know this is now the second time to say this, but wrongful accusations are often made, that is until we hit play back.

Nancy explained to Gabriel that friends don't hit friends. She also told him that she knew he was new to The Castle and may not know the rules. It was here that the strangest thing happened. Some of you might have experienced this too! Gabriel began to growl.

Nancy softly explained to him that she didn't speak "growl," and if he wanted to talk with her, he needed to speak "people talk."

To this, he growled out, "I can't because I have anger management issues."

"Who told you have anger management issues?"

Growling again, he said, "My mom and my teacher."

Again speaking softly, Nancy said, "I don't think that's true, you are too young to have anger management issues. What you have is a choice issue."

Gabriel stopped growling.

Nancy continued, "All you need to do is make better choices, choices not to be angry, not to get upset, and not to strike out."

She explained that he now had to choose between two new choices. One was to go to mom and dad and miss out on all the fun in The Castle. The second was to go back into The Castle, apologize to the little boy he punched, enjoy the rest of the service, and possibly win a prize.

He chose the latter.

Scripture tells us in Proverbs 15:1 (NLT):

> A gentle answer deflects anger,
> but harsh words make tempers flare.

As weeks and months passed, Gabriel came into The Castle and gave Nancy a thumbs-up gesture to signal that he was making great choices. He no longer had "anger management issues." As the years past in The Castle, Gabriel grew to be a very tall, handsome young man. He graduated to the youth department, but he always stopped by The Castle, with a thumbs-up for Nancy. A short time later, his parents moved and we didn't see Gabriel for four years.

One spring, a tall, handsome high-school senior walked into The Castle with his eyes fixed on Nancy. He stood there in the doorway and raised his hand as if to make a fist. But, in mid-motion, he slowly raised his thumb to indicate he was doing everything she had taught him, with a thumps-up, to show her that he was still making the best choices! I could see the tears of joy in both their eyes as they exchanged hugs. One of the most incredible blessings of being a children's pastor is watching your children grow and seeing their lives unfold with truth, grace, and the love of Christ.

Many times churches come up with a list of rules a mile long. They give children many rules and regulations to follow. They go as far as to print these rules on a large poster in the room, hoping the children will read and follow them. Most of the time, children glance at them occasionally, but there are so many rules, and there are so many things that children can do wrong, that these children's ministers spend so much time administering consequences that they tend to overlook what is causing a discipline issue to arise. In addition, these children's ministers never get to the reason why they are

Chapter Nine

there—to teach the love of God to young impressionable hearts.

A sample list of rules that I don't recommend follows. This is an actual list from a church we visited once:

Kids Church Rules
To show respect to our Heavenly Father and others:

1. Be Early
2. Be Respectful
3. Be Responsible
4. Be Reverent
    Stay in your seat
    Use your quiet voice
    Keep all your stuff under your chair
5. Be a Good Listner
    Raise your hand to talk
    Listen to the lesson
    Only one person talks at a time
6. Be Involved
7. Be Christlike

Read this list over two more times before you read on. How many rules do you remember?

We really need to "keep it simple and real" so that the rules are not difficult to remember, understand or keep. What is more important than the few rules you select are the need for children to have continuity and consistency. They should be able to know what to expect. We always keep services open to fun and with exciting differences, but always, quickly, we orally review the rules at the beginning of each service. This way, children know what is expected of them, even during their very first visit.

Why Do We Have Only Three Rules?

I remember early in our ministry, before I had learned what I am telling you now, we had a particular young man, age eight, named Jacob, who consistently broke the rules. Every Sunday and Wednesday, he would end up in the discipline area. When asked what the problem was, he would simply shrug his shoulders and then give us a blank look.

I asked him if he knew which rule he had broken.

He answered the same way every time shaking his head, "No." When pressed, he reluctantly told us that he didn't even know what the rules were.

I was shocked. In every service he had attended, we had diligently reviewed the rules. They were posted on every wall, in case someone forgot one. The rule list we used then came from another children's church in our home town. It was:

The "Be"havior List

Be early
Bring your Bible
Bring an offering
Be attentive
Be quiet
Be respectful
Be involved.

After each rule, we wrote a secondary rule that explained the main rule. We thought the best way for children to know the rules was to repeat them at every service. All we had were seven rules. Well, that's what we thought. Jacob taught us one of the most important lessons of our children's ministry careers. Instead of an endless list of dos and don'ts, we adopted the KISS approach: keep it simple, silly.

After a lot of prayer and a little help from an enormously

successful children's pastor, Willie George, we adopted the three rule system that we continue to use today and highly recommend to you. As stated previously, our children's church rules are:

1. Sit tall
2. Be quiet – listen
3. Participate

After almost thirty years of being away from our church, Jacob visited us in Fort Worth. He now had a young family, and they sat on the front row with excited looks on their faces. The praise and worship time of our service was incredibly awesome (as usual). Next, came the time to share the rules of children church. Without hesitation, Jacob excitedly threw his hands up and waited to be asked what the rules were. I could see his determination in giving the answers so why not let him share the rules—if he remembered them correctly. To my surprise, he perfectly recited each rule with great gusto and pride.

I doubt he remembered the first set of rules we had! In full, truthful disclosure, when I began writing this chapter, I even had to go back to some of our earlier notes to check what the first set of seven unsuccessful rules were! And yes, I keep all my notes from year to year. They help me visualize how far we've grown, and act as a valuable tool in directing us to where we are going.

Discipline in the Ranks

I have always been amazed at the effect children have on each other. One bad apple, as they say, can ruin a whole basket of good ones. On the other hand, one good youngster can change the attitudes of a whole classroom. Let me explain.

We use what we phrase "discipline in the ranks" as a

way to help produce the right atmosphere in our children's church. Over the years we have trained our older children to recognize problematic situations as they begin to unfold. For example, during praise and worship, the Holy Spirit moves and many members of our worship team are either perform on the platform or they walk through the crowd, meeting with children in need of prayer.

Not everyone feels the move of God during these times. Thus, they provide opportunities for small groups of children (usually boys) to let their attention wander from what's happening at the front. As these small groups begin to appear, our young leaders, who are always watching, begin to move in the direction of the problem. Most of the time, these leaders merely stand between the children who are not participating, physically encouraging them while using their modeling as examples to redirect their attention to the service.

If this doesn't work, they quietly ask them what they are supposed to be doing at that time. This method has been so incredibly successful in quelling problematic situations that we very rarely have issues with discipline during our services. We are always trained and ready to take care of anything that comes up. I am totally convinced that "discipline through the ranks" is one of the most important things you can do with your young leaders.

Some of the most effective services we ever had have been where children take over the service leading praise and worship, leading in the rules and offering, and also speaking to their peers. You can hear a pin drop during these times. A few adults occupy the room, but don't interfere with the flow unless things fall apart. They never have.

The big question is: how long do you have? This is not a sprint but a marathon. The vision or call for Nancy and I is to raise up a generation of children to take our place just as Jesus did with his small group. The body must go on.

Chapter Nine

In the summer of 2019, Nancy and I took our annual, two-week vacation, and instead of inviting an adult guest speaker, we literally left the children's church in the hands of our children's leadership team, the Knights. Two weeks, six services, and hundreds of children in the hands of nine, very anointed young people—I didn't have a single doubt that things would not go well.

Our team recorded the services on Facebook Live, and we watched the services from 1,400 miles away. Nancy and I rejoiced as we watched each service unfold and our team reached out touching the hearts of every child in attendance. I know many would shudder at the thought of doing this. I made sure we had the utmost confidence from our senior pastor, and assured there was adequate adult supervision before we set this in motion.

Such student leadership has taken us several years to bring to pass, training and mentoring children to become leaders who can take my place. In the past few years, our children's church has been totally kid led while Nancy, myself, and our adult team watch from just a few feet away. We feel so blessed to see how the Holy Spirit has empowered our young leaders.

So you ask, "Can this happen in my church?"

The answer is *yes*! You can do this too.

At What Age Can Children Learn to Worship?

> When Elizabeth heard Mary's greeting, the baby leaped in her womb, and Elizabeth was filled with the Holy Spirit (Luke 1:41 NIV).

John the Baptist, as an unborn child, jumped in his mother's womb when Mary, her cousin, came close. I believe this was a form of praise or even worship of the coming King because he felt the presence of Jesus, the Messiah. I think I would jump too! His mother, Elizabeth, was also instantly filled with the Holy Spirit, and spoke an amazing word over Mary.

Why did John jump for joy? Simple answer, he came within touching distance of God!

I have watched multitudes of children, of all ages, excitedly praise and worship the Father because we gave them the opportunity to come within touching distance of God, their Heavenly Father. We call this "face time with God." Children, as young as early childhood, dance with excitement during praise and worship portion of our service, or they stand with hands raised and eyes closed as they enter into their worship. Do you remember that moment in your life when you entered into your worship and tears began to flow as you fell to your knees before your Father?

Yes, I have heard the arguments of many well-meaning pastors and children's leaders who speak against giving children the opportunity to flow in praise and worship. My answer to these arguments is simple. Don't mock something until you have experienced it.

Look at what Jesus said of those who mocked the children who shouted praise in Matthew 21:14-16 (NIV):

> [14] The blind and the lame came to him at the temple, and he healed them. [15] But when the chief priests and the teachers of the law saw the wonderful things he did and the children shouting in the temple courts, "Hosanna to the Son of David," they were indignant.
> [16] "Do you hear what these children are saying?" they asked him.
> "Yes," replied Jesus, "have you never read,
>   'From the lips of children and infants
>   you, Lord, have called forth your praise.'"

I'm not going to argue with that, what about you? If Jesus recognized the potential for "perfected praise" in the hearts of children, shouldn't we do the same?

What Do You Do to Protect the Children and the Church from Abuse?

I believe that child abuse covers a lot of very delicate situations. Over the years, we have become more and more aware of the absolute need to protect our children. This is not a safe world in which children can grow without protection. There are dangers in every corner, making it a major miracle for a child to grow into adulthood! Just getting out of the womb intact in our modern world is a huge gamble.

Abortion rates soar, politicians, and Planned Parenthood all take their tolls as the fights rage on for the right to kill, not save, an innocent, unborn child. My heart breaks at the sheer numbers of pre-birth murders taking place in our "Christian nation" under the guise of women's rights. Our nation explodes with anger at the very thought of killing an exotic bird or near extinct animal, but the right to murder an innocent, unborn child is being touted as a basic human right. May God have mercy on us.

Today, some of the main reasons given to terminate an unborn child have been and still are, if the child interferes with the woman's education, or if the mother says: "I can't afford to raise a child", or "I'm not ready to be a mother", or many other multitudes of excuses. By the time a child enters our church, he or she has already overcome mountainous attacks and destructive situations to their welfare.

What do we do to put an end to this? We teach every child about the love of God. We start very young, from the moment they understand what a loving hug feels like. We teach them to feel the warmth of God's presence in worship.

We create an opportunity for them to build their relationship with God. We teach them the meaning of what is right and wrong, share godly morals and responsibility, and diligently pray that somewhere down their path they will live a life of righteousness; thus, avoiding the necessity of becoming a mother seeking to find a way out of her situation by aborting her own unwanted child.

Many Types of Child Abuse

Child abuse comes in many disguises from physical to mental, from social to spiritual. I have watched the world become plagued with an epidemic of child abuse, including children being beaten, ridiculed, set aside, and deprived of a savior. Children wander and grow up in a world filled with hate and anger. Other children are sexually abused, sometimes traded between family members and strangers as pawns or prizes.

Take Nicky, a six-year-old, who came to us in the middle of the night, dressed in a baby doll nightie and pink underwear. (Nancy and I were registered as a CHINA [Child In Need Of Assistance] Petition home.) Under the cover of night, we met with police and social workers on a deserted parking lot to pick up what we thought was a little, six-year old girl. Nicky turned out to be a little boy, with long black hair and a look of fear on his face.

Just an hour before, he had been used as a sexual pawn during a game of Dungeons & Dragons with his drug-abusing mother and boyfriend. Having been passed around for the players' depraved gratification, Nicky was left with deep scars both physically, mentally, and emotionally. His nights were filled with demons and evil spirits pounding on his bedroom window. His days were filled with the absolute distrust of any male person. Remember, he was only six.

I want to share a second example from the time four-year-

Chapter Nine

old Joshua came to our church for the first time. He was a bright-eyed blonde with a smile a mile wide. His dad dropped him off at our preschool department with a warning to the teacher that if he acted up, she was to let him know. The father would take care of it on the way home.

That warning was not all his father gave. He turned to Joshua and said, "This is just in case you forget to behave while I'm gone," and he drew back and slapped Joshua across the face. This left both a red mark and a little boy screaming his heart out. Stunned and appalled, the worker called us to the room while Joshua continued screaming.

We were present when the parents came back to get Joshua who was still sobbing from the blow earlier. He was very reluctant to leave the room. This incident happened over thirty years ago. Recently, we read in a news report that Joshua, as a teenager, had been arrested for murder. I know this is an extreme case of child abuse, but I remember telling his parents, on numerous occasions, they needed to get help with their parenting skills while there was still time because one day Joshua would grow up and be strong enough to bench press a pick-up truck. He would eventually fight back against the violence he was enduring. Sadly, even reporting this situation to authorities had no effect. Joshua's parents had refused any kind of counseling or help from the church.

So, what can the church do to counter the abuse aimed at children? These are the five steps that we take and recommend to you:

1. Pray for wisdom and guidance;
2. Provide a safe and wholesome environment for all children to enjoy as they find their forever home in the family of God;
3. Train all workers, volunteers, and church members to recognize the signs of abuse;

4. Set up reporting protocols, i.e., who, when, what, and how to report abuse; and,
5. Follow up with every child and their families.

Testimony of Carl Pedida

Throughout my time in the Knights, I have had many mentors. Each modeled a different concept or helped me develop a new skill. Sometimes they taught me something about music and/or a new musical technique. Other times they explained what the heart of worship was to them, how to worship on stage, or how to create new sound booth queues. All my mentors loved getting into specifics. A great thing about Knight Mentors is they could (and probably would) become one of your closest friends while you were learning under them.

I have also learned that when you are a Knight, "People will be watching you." Younger kids will be looking up to us [—just like Gian's own "knight in shining armor" in Chapter Seven].

The great thing about the first generation of Knights was that they set a precedent for what future generations should be. This standard provides the present Knights with a set of guidelines about how to be a good role model. We inspire younger children to become a Knight because they see Jesus in us. Also, when you get a reputation as a leader in children's ministry, people are going to watch you and unconsciously (or consciously) wait for a slip-up. That puts heavy, but very much needed pressure on the Knights. It's that pressure that moves us to do better and to prevail against all opposition.

As KOGs, we are motivated to chase after the goals and the blessings that the Lord has set before us. If it wasn't for the Knights, we would never cherish every experience with God the way we do now. We probably wouldn't even understand the concept of unity as well as we do right now. We would have

Chapter Nine

no reason to be better people. If it wasn't for The Knights, our true walks with God would probably be starting about now as teenagers (or Lord forbid, even later). The KOGs, Pastor Ray, and Mrs. Nancy have given us an opportunity to be closer to our God. And for that, we're eternally grateful.

— Carl Pedida
Current KOG Member

BEGIN THE CHANGE NOW

If you are a children's minister, we recommend that you establish safety protocols to protect your children. If you need direction in this area, we recommend that you, your workers and your church pastors visit the MinistrySafe website (ministrysafe.com), and research what it would take for your church to become a safe place for children and families.

As a children's minister, we suggest that you offer Christian parenting classes as often as possible to help educate and train young parents on how to raise godly Children.

Now that you have read our suggestions on discipline, we ask you to review your list of rules and simplify it down to three. Train all your young youth leaders and adult volunteers on how to use our three-step redirection procedure to turn discipline challenges into teachable moments. After this training has been completed, identify youth in your group who are gifted to become leaders of your "discipline in the ranks" program.

As children's ministers, we encourage you to keep all your notes from year to year, and review them when you are planning the direction for a new year. Remember that to change the ways you do things. Pray earnestly, seek God's plan, use your God-given imagination, and walk one step at a time, in faith, as you venture out in search of a better plan.

If you are a parent, find out if your church has safety protocols in place to protect your child(ren). If not, encourage your church to look into providing training for all their workers and staff. Also, do you remember that moment in your life when you entered into worship and tears began to flow as you fell to your knees before the Father? If so, describe that moment to your child(ren). Ask them to share when they have felt close enough to God that they could touch Him. If you do not remember such an event, pray and ask the Holy Spirit to lead you into a deeper relationship with Him.

Lastly, all of us as parents wish that our child(ren) had come with an instructional manual! All of us seek to be the best possible parents at all times. The Bible serves as our guide. You may also feel that you need additional help. You may want to ask your pastors about books or classes that teach parenting skills. We know that you were disturbed by the stories about parental neglect in this chapter. We know your pastors will have resources to offer for your guidance, or for you to offer to other parents so that such stories do not occur again.

Chapter Ten

HOW TO BEGIN A CHILDREN'S MINISTRY, PART THREE

Comments & Questions Heard from Senior Pastors, Children's Workers & Parents

P roverbs 19:18 (ISV) tells us to:

> Discipline your son while there is still hope—but don't set your heart on his destruction.

Many misunderstand this scripture and think it means to beat your children into submission. How wrong they are. Ephesians 6:4 (NIV) gives us a better look at the way we should raise our children:

> Fathers, do not exasperate your children; instead, bring them up in the training and instruction of the Lord.

There are so many stories, scenarios, and tragedies in the lives of children that we must have a strategic plan to keep them safe. Please understand that we simply cannot just pray and leave it there. We must be proactive in creating a safe environment in our churches. We must develop programs that provide information so children learn how to recognize the warning signals of potential danger. We must constantly educate our workers and staff to all these dangers as well. They must be able to see the telltale signs that communicate when a child has been abused or are still enduring abuse. So where do we start.

Single Parents

According to Wikipedia, in the United States today, there are nearly 13.6 million single parents raising over 21 million children.[15] Marriage rates over the past two decades have dropped from 9.8 to 7.3 per thousand.[16] My heart goes out to single parents who work ungodly hours, struggling to raise their children.

I vividly remember such a young mom in one of our first churches. She came to church seeking a place to fit in. She also needed encouragement as she attempted to raise her young son. She lived in a rented garage that had been equipped with a bathroom and small cook stove. They had one bed, very little furniture, but their garage "bed-sit" was always spotless. She worked two jobs, one during the day when her son was at kindergarten and a second one at night that allowed her to take him with her. It would be an understatement to say her life was hard. The heartbreak of her situation drew us into her life. Mikey, her "little man," was her entire life. Her every waking moment was spent loving him and caring for his every need. She found Christ her very first church visit. She found the real reason to work hard. It changed her life.

I listed this example first because the vast majority of children who are abused by predators tend to come from single parent homes. Because of this, in our ministry, we endeavor

Chapter Ten

to provide the strongest support to single parents, both educationally and socially. Throughout the week, our church hosts a number of programs, including *Celebrate Recovery*, *Man Church*, and *Kingdom Women*. For the children we have *DC4Kids* (*DivorceCare* for Kids). We also have qualified men and women who are mentors for children being raised in single parent homes. We educate and train all of our workers through a program called MinistrySafe, mentioned in the last chapter, which is an intense, child sexual abuse awareness program—more on this later.

Divorce

According to Wikipedia, divorce rates have also dropped over the last two decades from 4.7 to 3.6 per thousand.[17] This does not mean that marriages are on the rise. Just the opposite. We are becoming a nation of unmarried, single parents, setting a trend for future generations to emulate. Children of divorce are often angry, hurt, and confused when their parents separate and later divorce.

For example, one nine-year-old boy sank to the carpet sobbing during one of our children's church praise and worship services. Several of our young leaders knelt by his side and prayed for him. He was inconsolable and could not be comforted. During the time for sharing that day, he came to the microphone, and simply said, "I caused my parents to divorce."

His words struck many hearts, especially those who were from single parent homes. Many children believe that they caused their parents separation, and this blame is a deep-cutting heartache.

DC4K, or *DivorceCare* for Kids, is a safe and fun, weekly activity for ages seven to twelve. In this program, children learn skills to help them heal. *DC4K* groups blend a variety of activities, including games, music, stories, videos, and discussions to help hurting children deal with the effects of divorce and to move forward.

Poverty

In a study by The National Center for Children in Poverty (NCCP), it was determined that "[a]bout 15 million children in the United States—21 percent of all children—live in families with incomes below the federal poverty threshold." [18] This measurement has even underestimated the needs of these families.[19] "Research shows that, on average, families need an income of about twice [the designated American poverty] level to cover basic expenses."[20] This study went on to state that 43 percent of American children live in low-income families.[21] Thus, hunger and poverty are not just a third-world country problem. They surround us on every street corner in America.

As a child, I grew up in a very poor family. My parents had fourteen children. My mom gave birth to four sets of twins. I was one of them. We grew up not having everything we needed or wanted. Most of the time, I grew up in ignorance, not knowing what it meant to "have enough." I remember, more than I care to admit, the number of times I was sent around the corner to ask a neighbor for a half-crown—the equivalence of about one American dollar. The excuse was to go buy bread to feed everyone. The real reason was that my folks had run out of money for cigarettes. Yes, we got bread, but the first item was always a pack of Woodbines. I knew what it was to eat cabbage in every form possible. Despite the instances we went without electricity—because the power was turned off—there was always a smell of cigarettes in the house.

Every Friday, payday came around, and we ate high on the hog, or so we thought. We ate bread with crab paste, corned beef, and carrots. Saturday morning we—and I mean all the

Chapter Ten

kids—loaded onto a city bus with mom, and headed to the market where she bought a leg of lamb and something called "neck ends." To this day, I still have no idea what a "neck end" is. All of us shared shoes (without socks), pants, and shirts. Two in a bed at night was the total amount of privacy afforded. We bathed once a week in a tub that was filled only once for the entire family.

I know what poverty is. I have a very clear picture of what it means to have nothing to eat but dry crust, toasted on an open fire with "beef dripping" spread on it for lunch. I know, that sounds delicious, right? *Wrong*. Most of the time it was disgusting, but it was all I had to eat.

My parents did the best they could. Both worked every hour they could. Dad worked in the local brick factory, and Mom in the local cotton mill. As my siblings and I grew, we all had jobs well before the time that we left school. I knew what it meant to be without, and yet I never knew a time when I didn't feel loved and wanted. I had the best childhood. My childhood was an adventure, experienced only by those who have nothing. I wrote about many of these adventures in a series of exciting short stories, which I have read and told to thousands of children throughout Texas starting in the nineties.

For me, poverty was both a blessing and a curse. I totally understand it, what causes it, what promotes it, and what transpires from it. I am thankful for all the life lessons I learned as a child. They have made me who I am today. When I found Christ, I found abundance "more than enough." I have never needed or wanted for anything since. I can say with certainty that the Lord is faithful.

> I was young once and now I am old,
>   yet I have never seen the righteous forsaken
>   or their children begging bread
>   (Ps 37:25 NIV).

This Psalm is one of the driving forces that make it imperative that we reach and teach every child who crosses our paths. They all need a savior who can provide all their needs according to His riches in glory.

Over the years we have been, and are still, involved with several programs to help children raised in poverty. *Project Joy* is a program that operates around Christmas time to provide food, clothing, and gifts for underprivileged children and their families. *Shoes for Kids* and *Coats for Kids* take place around early fall to provide shoes and coats for children as they enter school. These programs continue well into the winter months. Check your local ministerial alliance for information about these, and other community projects, or simply research the needs around you and start your own program.

In addition to poverty, the world around us deals with an ever-increasing number of child endangerment issues. These include school shootings, sexual abuse, abduction, and human trafficking. I heard that in America alone, a child goes missing every four minutes! We cannot let this trend continue.

When we became the parents of two little boys, our lives changed forever. Our lives were now all about raising them. Not only were we parents and providers, but also protectors. These last few decades have proven to be the most devastating of all for child abduction and school/church shootings. Social media, local and national news are ablaze with the latest disappearances or attacks on the innocent.

Once, while sitting in a children's ministry planning meeting, with a dozen or so children's workers, the meeting was abruptly fractured by an all too familiar screech on almost everyone's phone announcing the latest Amber Alert. Often, even teaching "stranger danger" techniques seems like a wasted effort in the light of so many missing children. But, we cannot stop instructing our wide-eyed youngsters on who to talk to and who to trust.

Chapter Ten

As a result, we talk about safety in our children's church every month or so. We encourage our parents to do the same. We enthusiastically train our workers to recognize "stranger danger" and to always be on the lookout for any situation that doesn't look right. We vigorously screen all our staff and volunteers. In some cases, just the training itself weeds out those who would throw up a red flag.

One of the most important aspects in keeping our children safe is that we know our children. We watch for changes in their behavior patterns. For instance, a child who once was very active but now crouches in a corner away from everyone is a signal to us of a potential change in that child's life outside of our church. If a child who was once quiet and unassuming is now striking out at other children, this is another red flag. If a child who is an A student but begins to fail, we know we need to show concern. All of these and more are red flags that something has happened, and we need to find out as much as we can to help create a safe environment for that child.

Several years ago, a little girl—who was very outgoing, always sat on the front row, and danced to the music—began to retreat into a corner. She stopped speaking to anyone. Nancy noticed this change almost immediately, but this little one would not share what her heavy heart was hiding. Weeks went by and then her little brother began to show similar changes in behavior. We tried talking with their mom, but she was not forthcoming either. Then, just days later, in the middle of our summer camp in East Texas, this troubled youngster opened up to her favorite counselor.

Tears flowed and would not stop. She told her counselor what had been happening in her home. Nancy was close by and saw the intense look on the young counselor's face, so she stepped in to listen. Once the initial ice had been broken, her brother also shared the dangers and violence that was occurring. Please forgive the fact that I will not be sharing the horrific details of this case, but so many of these cases are filled with terrible stories and lifelong traumatized victims.

In Texas, we have a law where everyone is a "Mandatory Reporter" when a child is in harm's way. No matter what we think or feel about what we hear, if a child is in danger of being hurt, we must report the instance we observed to child welfare and/or the local police. In the case described before as well as in many others we have experienced, we first called the children's mother who was, according to her children, also being abused. We asked her what was happening in her home, but the mom still refused to talk. Our next phone call that day, after much prayer and discussion with our senior pastor, was to Child Protective Services.

The positive note to this story is that the child and her brother are now on the road to healing. Suffice to say, due to our intervention, these children were given a safe environment, after months of counseling. Yes, the family broke up, but it was severely broken long before we became involved. Over the next few months, mom and her children found help physically, socially, and spiritually to overcome their times of need.

Let me say this also: almost every time we have taken steps like we did in the story above because a child is being harmed, sadly, the family often leaves the church due to embarrassment or anger because we stepped in. This responsibility is one of the most difficult aspects of our ministry and causes much distress, but it is also one that is so important. We have grown to know how to help and minister to hurting families during these times. We have learned how to advise and walk through the processes as they unfold, while realizing, at the same time, the church may lose the family we are helping.

When we first opened up our own summer camp, called *SureWord Pioneer Summer Camp* (held deep in the piney woods of East Texas), our first step, when creating this safe, summer camp environment, was to call Attorney Gregg Love with

Chapter Ten

MinistrySafe for advice and training. That was over twenty-five years ago. We still use MinistrySafe to train our staff and volunteers on strategies to keep our children, staff, and church safe from any, and all, outside influences that have evil intent.

School and Church Shootings

Society has a mindset that churches are safe places where children and families will be protected from the outside insanity. The last forty years, however, have proven this perception to be untrue. What do we do to provide the safest environment possible? We educate and train all of our staff and volunteers. Even our church members who are "pre-volunteers" are encouraged to attend these trainings.

Yes, we also have uniformed police at every major entrance. You might say, "Wow, that's a bit harsh," but let me share with you the comments of two families—one comes from a mother with three young children who came to our program for the first time:

> I'm so thankful there is a police officer on duty at the South entrance. That makes me feel so much better about leaving my children in The Castle and heading to the adult sanctuary.
>
> What a blessing to be able to attend church and know that every member of my family has a safe place to worship. —*from a longtime member*

Here's the exciting part! Almost every officer who has taken time to be on duty with us has given their hearts to the Lord, and they now serve in our church. One of them, Sergeant (Sgt.) Kovar now leads our men's ministry with a passion to reach men. Another great by-product of our safety program is that children get to interact with a uniformed police officer in a positive way. Instead of fearing the police, they gain a respect and trust for the uniform. For example, one Wednesday evening we asked Sgt. Kovar to speak to the children in The Castle about what he does. He shared his love for his service to his community and what it means to "serve and protect." He shared several times that he was one of the good guys!

He fielded dozens of questions from very excited children. At the end of Sgt. Kovar's talk, the children gathered around him and began to pray for him (as well as the men and women who served alongside him). As each child prayed, I watched tears flow down his face with gratitude for their prayers, and the knowledge that there are now young hearts lifting him and his colleagues up to the Father. The children left with a new idea and a new understanding of what a police officer is: they are the good guys!

The power of a child's prayer; *#childrenbehindtheshield*.

We also have deacons at every entrance and several who walk the hallways during every service. In addition, there are deacons in every major ministry of our church who serve in their ministry, including children's ministry. Moreover, we follow the procedures in our Emergency Procedures Manual, and often practice fire, tornado and lockdown drills. The children love it when they hear the alarm fire up! Most have learned what it means, and follow all verbal instructions.

I know this seems a bit much just to attend church but this is not the days of "Ozzie and Harriet" or "Father Knows Best." But, we are open! At our church, our doors are not open at all hours of the day and night. Times have changed, and sadly not for the better. Therefore, our program has changed with

Chapter Ten

the times. Out of necessity, we look for better ways to enjoy our time of praise and worship with our families in safety.

I have a question for you. Do you have an Emergency Procedures Manual for your church? If not, why not? The manual is not just for when a problem emerges; it's to be used regularly. Be proactive, be ready, and be prepared. Your church families deserve it and will appreciate it. We simply cannot stand by idly and watch generations of children fall by the wayside as we sing our cute, little action songs.

MinistrySafe

Earlier, I stated that we use MinistrySafe. We require all our staff and volunteers to be trained and educated through this abuse prevention system. MinistrySafe provides churches with a comprehensive system of resources that assist in the design and implementation of safety systems throughout the church and throughout all of our ministries on or off site. This prevention training helps reduce the risk of sexual abuse of children, youth, and other vulnerable people in our ministries.

According to MinistrySafe, this system includes the following foundational components:

- A MinistrySafe policy, put in effect in each congregation;
- Volunteer/staff screenings, including a standardized application, interview and reference check process for potential new church personnel;
- Criminal background checks for volunteers/staff;
- Online training for volunteers/staff;
- A unique control panel for each church to assist in record keeping during each part of the process, including an automatic notification of the need to renew training; and,
- Monitoring tools for periodic review of the system.

We have used this system for many years. I can say without a shadow of doubt that we have averted some devastating situations because we had MinistrySafe in place. Many times when adults come and ask to work in our children's ministry, we have recognized red flags because of this training. Some even immediately withdraw their application when they realize we have a system that teaches us to recognize child predators.

The church is most vulnerable, and more often than not, openly willing to accept any and all volunteers who have a desire to minister to young people. We deal with literally hundreds of children on a daily basis, and see the potential disasters in both adult and youth behaviors as other churches walk around with blinders on, believing that everyone is intrinsically good and wouldn't harm a fly in God's house.

I highly recommend MinistrySafe to you as a must-have safety training program for your church. Through this system, your pastors, office staff, teachers, and volunteers will be well equipped to deal with situations that arise. This training results in your children and youth being kept safe, and your ongoing church ministry is secured for generations to come.

"Where Should I Look for the Right Person to Lead the Children?"

My answer to this question has always been in-house. If there is a person already in your church who has been attending for some time, it's always better to check them out first. They are already aware of the church's vision and the senior pastor's heart. These are super important aspects of children's ministry leadership and will save the church so much time when it comes to training the right person. Make sure your church's vision, mission statement, and the senior pastor's vision for the church are written down. You are sure to need these items in your search for the right person.

Chapter Ten

In every children's pastor's position I have taken, there were only two in which my wife and I were totally unaware of the pastors' heart or vision for the church. After several long meetings, we began to get the feel of where the pastor wanted to go with children's ministry and what he expected from us. Many times a Senior Pastor doesn't have a clear picture of what it takes to either create a children's ministry or how it should be run.

The idea that Sunday school—what most senior pastors think of when they hear children's ministry—is "the be-all and end-all" to children's ministry can be very misleading. Sunday school has begun to take a back seat to children's church, or at best, it has partnered with children's church to reach and educate the children in spiritual matters. The senior pastor's vision for his children's department will determine the type of leader you need to seek.

One day, a dear friend, and fellow children's pastor, called me. She had moved from her former church to take over a much larger children's ministry. Her heart overflowed with amazing ideas, and she exploded into her new church with energy and enthusiasm. Yet, after six months in her new position, she felt as if she is being stifled. She has not been able to fit into the pastor's vision for his church. Her Pastor simply wanted a vibrant Sunday school, not a children's church.

Since my dear friend is all about both teaching children in class and giving them the ability to experience God's presence in a kids' church setting, she has found the road ahead very rocky and filled with disappointment. So with humility and sincerity, we strongly recommend that you find out what your senior pastor's vision is before you jump in headlong

First, look to your local congregation for leadership, check out young couples who enjoy volunteering in the children's ministry. Ask if there are any adults who are led to work with children, and investigate each of their abilities and gifts.

Second, ask other children's pastors for referrals. Over the years we have trained many young people and couples who are very adept at ministry for children. There are others out there, like us, who train and mentor young leaders. I am constantly hearing from people who are a part of KidMin—an organization of children ministers—looking for new adventures in ministry. There are also several sites online who advertise ministry opportunities for all levels of ministry. Try:

>indeed.com/hire/Pastor
>childrensministryonline.com
>ChurchStaffing.com

or simply do a search yourself. There are many sites out there.
Third, pray earnestly! Follow God!

"What Should I Look for in a Children's Pastor?"

I have found that the best children's pastors share the following six characteristics.

1. **They are men/women who are deeply devoted to God.** I like the way Titus 1:6-7 (NIV) responds to the question of what to look for in a Children's Pastor:

    > 6 An elder [in this case a children's pastor] must be blameless, faithful to his wife, a man whose children believe and are not open to the charge of being wild and disobedient.
    > 7 Since an overseer manages God's household, he must be blameless—not overbearing, not quick-tempered, not given to drunkenness, not violent, not pursuing dishonest gain.

Chapter Ten

If these men and women are a husband/wife team, or husband or wife, they should have their own homes in order. They should have well-disciplined children.

2. **They should be people who are not on their way to a higher calling.** It's a sad truth that many children and youth pastors are really not in it for the long haul. Many are simply using these ministries as a stepping stone to something better.

   I was sixty-seven years old when I began writing this book. I have been asked more times than I care to count, "How come you're still in children's ministry? Why haven't you moved up to become a senior pastor by now?" That's a great question and I'm sure that many people think that being a children's minister is the first step on the obvious path into senior ministry, but not me.

   I started out wanting to be in children's ministry, but, due to pressure from my district superintendent in Iowa—who said quite adamantly, "That's a waste of your education!"—Nancy and I agreed to take on a senior pastor's position in a small, but struggling church. Three churches later, with the last church teeming with children, it became quite obvious that our calling in life was with children. Look for someone who is *called* to children's ministry.

3. **They must have integrity.** Integrity matters and is extremely important. Children's pastors need to be people of integrity, honesty, fairness, stick by their word, say what they mean and mean what they say. Children need this kind of example in their lives, because for the most part many do not have this type of example in their homes.

4. **They must be willing to submit to the senior pastor's vision.** They need to know and understand the senior

pastor's vision and heart. They need to submit to that vision; they are not to become rouge vigilantes trying to undermine what the church is.
5. **They must have a personal vision.** They need to have an idea of what children's ministry is. They need the ability to cultivate a vision that enables them to grow a church from the nursery up.
6. **They must love children.** I have met so many, well-meaning men and women who, due to a need in the children's department, either felt like they needed to fill the position or were cudgeled into taking it. Either way, their efforts never amounted to much in the Kingdom, with the exception of simply driving young people far from the church. A children's pastor who loves children will be much like a Pied Piper. They will have children flocking to them wherever they go.

When Nancy and I go shopping, it's not unusual for children to follow us or simply watch us from afar. We have actually had parents come up to us and ask who we are. It's the same in the elementary schools where we volunteer. Children seem to be mysteriously drawn to us. I believe there is a specific anointing for children's pastors. It acts like a bright flower to a honey bee. Children know they can trust you. They know that you care for them. They are drawn to you. You are a safe place for them.

Last comment we would like to discuss is also probably the one that is the most often asked: "But, we have always had a Sunday school."

My answer to this comment, every time, is: "How's that working for you?"

Refer back to Chapter One.

Chapter Ten

Testimony of Logan MacIntosh

Imagine a program completely different from any other children's ministry —teaching kids to spread the gospel and use the Holy Spirit! This is exactly what the Knights of God (KOG) do! They are an important part of our church because their unforgettable services inspire children to become worship leaders.

The KOGs cannot be compared with other ministries as they offer something completely different: face time with the Creator. This is what sets them apart as they create an environment of worship, drawing children into the presence of God. Normally people think of children's ministry as a Sunday school where kids color worksheets, watch old movies, and have snack time! The Knights don't need any of those things to have a great service. The Knights of God take advantage of the little time that they have during each service, leading kids into a deep, meaningful relationship with God through worship. Most people that see the Knights for the first time are shocked as they haven't experienced anything like it before. Because of this uniqueness, the Knights will always be something to remember.

The KOG inspire and raise up children to become great worship leaders. They are always looking for new members. As time passes and the current Knights get older, they eventually become interested in other ministry teams in the church. Consequently, the Knights are constantly training and leading children to become the next, adult worship leaders. Approximately eight years ago, I walked into the Castle for the first time and was instantly captivated. I envisioned myself leading worship with the Knights someday. After a few years of guitar lessons and commitment, I now help to lead worship every week. This has been the case with other Knights as well.

The KOGs cultivate a life-changing environment, and they are always raising up children to become future leaders. This is why the Knights of God are, and always will be, deeply valuable and meaningful to our church ministry and will always be an overall influence to all they meet.

—**Logan MacIntosh**
KOG Member

BEGIN THE CHANGE NOW

If you are a children's minister, be certain that your ministry has an Emergency Procedures Manual and write one if you do not. Practice fire and safety drills every six months with your children. Also, during these moments of safety reviews, emphasize "stranger danger" rules of who to talk to and who to trust. Implement MinistrySafe if you have not already done so. When the need arises in your church or other churches, follow our steps presented in this chapter to find an outstanding children's pastor.

If you are a parent, every month review with your children the safety rules that you want them to follow when they are with you and when they are away from home. Tell them the reasons behind each rule. By reminding them of the reasons why they cannot cross the street without you, for instance, in a quiet conversation, you will not have to raise your voice and scold your child in public. Ensure that they know "stranger danger" rules, what to do in case your home fire alarm system goes off, etc. By scheduling such meetings after family Bible study, you will enable your children to receive the added benefit of feeling the presence of God as a safe keeper in their lives.

Chapter Eleven

IF YOU CAN READ, YOU CAN DO ANYTHING

Children's Missions and Outreach

Missions are an essential part of ministry. One common phrase the Knights always remember is the real way to spell ministry: W-O-R-K. The Knights participate in mission trips. They do so to raise up and inspire other ministry teams so they that can recreate the same successes that our home church enjoys. For example, when the Knights went to Journey Church in Bozeman, Montana, we did just that! We spent two weeks worshiping, praying, and fellowshiping alongside their youth ministry team. By the end of our visit, these two ministry teams joined together to lead worship for the entire children's ministry. As a result, new Knights were knighted in Bozeman! Experiences like this also serve to bring the Knights closer together and make them a tighter team. They become more focused upon bringing the presence of God to new people.

Mission trips are also an excellent means of bringing the Knights closer to each other. In the example above, after spending two weeks together, they became a very tight-knit group. The Knights spent day after day in fellowship and worship together throughout the entire trip. This proved fruitful after we returned home. They realized they were closer to each other than they had ever been because of their worship and work for Journey Church.

The Knights have also been blessed with an incredible gift of drawing children into the presence of God. Taking our gifts to the mission field of our younger generation not only shares these amazing gifts with others, but strengthens and encourages our team to go and do it again and again. Have you worshiped at the feet of your Creator? Maybe you should come to a Knights service and see for yourself the awesomeness in the presence of our Almighty God!

Another important outreach program we commit to began when the schools in our community opened for the fall semester. Excitement and disappointment was the order of the day as we waited at the front door of our local elementary school on the red carpet for students to arrive. Some very excited children almost ran to be greeted by teachers, staff, local police, school officials, and us. The girls' hairdos were neatly tied with ribbons and sparkles; and, the boys' hair were slicked down without a strand out of place. New Spider-Man backpacks, flashing new tennis shoes, even creases in tan pants and shirts were the attire for the day.

A few tears from moms as they waved goodbye to their tiny kindergartners, and several dads carrying their little ones on their shoulders completed the picture. We gave high fives and fist bumps, and received hugs from returning students. Of course, there were a few who were absolutely unhappy about summer being over. They dreaded the thought of walking through the doors, and once again spend their days inside with books, pencils, homework, and rules.

Nancy and I have been involved with local schools for more than forty years. We first served as "classroom mom and dad" for both our children, and then as volunteers, substitute teachers, storytellers, and as community involvement volunteers with various activities. We have served on various committees including the Campus Performance Objective Committee (CPOC), Parents Assisting Whitehouse Schools (PAWS), and the Parent-Teacher Association (PTA) for years.

In 1994, we received the Friend of Education Award from the Whitehouse Independent School District, and then in 1995, we received the statewide Friend of Education Award from the Texas Classroom Teachers Association. I was honored to be named "Texan of the Week" by KLTV Channel 7 News, October 1999, for all that we do in our local schools and community. So, when I hear my fellow ministers and school officials tell me that the church is simply not allowed in the local school system, I just smile. We have never been denied entrance into any school district or classroom. We receive lots of invitations to come to schools all over Texas.

For example, in the first, second, and third grades at an elementary school in Whitehouse, Texas we started a program called *Much To Do About Reading* with the slogan, "if you can read, you can do anything." We met with the children once a week for story time. We read books with great moral significance, teaching the children about, honesty, respect, obedience, and the difference between right and wrong. Nancy, along with Much, her purple puppet (shown in Chapter One), brought laughter and taught morality throughout each story. For the third graders, we told more stories than read them. The children's favorite was the retelling of the book *Turkeys and Eagles* by Peter Lord. Over a six-week period, I created fantastic chalk pictures on the classroom board, and imaginary ones were pictured in the children's minds as we told this and other stories. We also encouraged the children to read at least one book a week and even write their own adventure stories.

For a second example, for almost twenty years, we shared stories at Mozelle Brown and Higgins Elementary Schools in Whitehouse, Texas. We often taught five classes at a time by meeting either in large classroom or by taking over the library.

We looked forward to these days with great anticipation, carefully crafting the right stories for the season. Children were always so excited when we arrived with Much, and, as one teacher put it, school attendance was almost always 100 percent on the days that we came.

We have heard repeatedly from children's pastors that they just don't have the time, or the inclination, to go to their local elementary schools and try to work their way in. I have to say there is no better place anywhere on the planet to have a more obedient, captive audience who is so hungry for what we have to offer.

One Friday morning, as we walked into one of our classrooms, we noticed that we were already being welcomed by dozens of smiling faces. We also saw, however, that one the little girls was unhappy and not participating. Her head hung low and she was crumpled in the back of the room. This was so unlike her. Her teacher informed us that she was not feeling well, but she didn't want to miss school that day because we would be there.

Nancy approached her asking what was wrong. She said she had tummy cramps and hadn't eaten anything that morning.

To our surprise, when Nancy asked if there was anything she could do for her, the little girl said, "If you say the words you say, I know I will feel better."

So, Nancy quietly whispered a short prayer in her ear, gave her a hug, and then made her way back to the front of the room. Everyone, even the children, knew we were children's pastors, so it made sense that she would ask for prayer, and it worked. By the end of class, she was sitting with a bright smile on her face. After this incident, we became well acquainted with this little one and visited her home many times.

We often remind teachers to try to get to find out about their students' home lives as they try to help the children learn. What follows is an example of why this is so important.

Chapter Eleven

One day, teacher said that Sarah had the wrong signature on her spelling list. Sarah was in third grade. To look at her, you would think this little one was from the very poorest of the poor. Her hair was never brushed, and her mismatched clothing was both dirty and unkempt. She was loud and often obnoxious. She always sat in the back of the class. That day, shortly after attendance, she was already outside the classroom with her nose to the wall crying. When Nancy saw her, she stopped to ask what the problem was.

"My teacher says that I signed my spelling papers instead of my mom, but I didn't."

Nancy hugged her and we went into the classroom. When Nancy commented to the teacher that the little girl was crying, she said, "Well, Sarah is out there because she is signing her own spelling papers instead of having her mom do it."

We arranged with the teacher that if it was okay with her, we would stop by, and have her mom sign the papers. So, later that afternoon we did.

Sarah and her little brother lived in a shambles of a home in the worst part of town. I could go into detail and describe it, but you wouldn't believe me. It was awful. She slept with her brother on a wooden pallet close to a Ben Franklin stove in the winter with old sleeping bags for cover. There was electricity and water, but no indoor bathroom. The floor was now dirt, though a remnant of the carpet remained in one corner under the almost spotless TV. The broken down furniture faced the TV as if bowing to a god.

Sitting endlessly staring at the mindless clatter spewing from the thirty-inch, color Magnavox was her mom clasping the remote. With her clothes in rags and chipped coffee mug in hand, she never once looked away to talk to, or greet her children when they came home. We spoke, informing her we had taken them home after school because her daughter had not been feeling well. Mom never once asked how she was;

she just shushed us mumbling that her show was on.

After the show was over, we found out that Sarah's mom only had a second grade education and never really learned how to write. The signatures on the papers were indeed hers. The next day we reported back to the teacher whose heart was crushed to think that she had jumped to the wrong conclusion and harshly disciplined Sarah.

"It all makes so much sense now as I look back at Sarah's homework," her teacher responded. This was a tough lesson to learn. Sarah was a product of her home life in more ways than one. Her lack of sleep, poor nutrition, and parental support in her education took quite a toll on her grades. Fortunately, now her teacher was equipped with information that helped her mentor and educate with greater results. The teacher told us, at the end of the year, that she now knows her students so well she doesn't want to let them move up to the next grade at the end of the year.

As children's pastors, Nancy and I couldn't walk away without doing all we could to assist Sarah, but mom wouldn't give us permission to help that day. Over the next few months, we assisted this poverty-stricken family with food, clothing, and bicycles for the children. Twin beds were placed carefully in this tiny, rundown home. We even spent several days repairing the doors, broken windows, and the kitchen sink, after we located it under a mountain of trash. We watched over the next year as these children began to flourish and grow; even their grades improved. Mom, however, proved to be the most difficult to help. We were never fully able to wean her from her shows. Both Sarah and her brother began to attend our *Kidz-Turn* children's ministry. After attending summer camp that year, they gave their lives to the Lord and I got to baptize them a few weeks later. God is so good.

This is just one of many families we met while at our local elementary schools, who we never knew existed nor would

Chapter Eleven

have known had we not been involved. We vividly recall one afternoon when our boys got off the school bus, and hurried into the house toward their bedrooms. From there, they bound into the kitchen, where they raided the refrigerator and pantry for snacks, which was not unusual. What was highly unusual that day was that they wanted to eat their snacks in their bedrooms, and get started on their homework.

Nancy walked back to check on them. She found a school friend with them. He was unwashed, poorly dressed, and had a bad odor. Our boys often brought a friend home, but only after arrangements had been made with their parents. On this occasion, there had been no arrangements.

Questions began that needed to be answered. Who was he? Where did he live? Did his parents know where he was?

Our boys said nothing at first, and then suddenly came a flood of answers. We were able to gather enough information that led us to one of the most heartbreaking encounters in our ministry. Our first thought was to call his mom. We couldn't do that because they didn't have a phone. So we loaded everyone in our station wagon and headed to the boy's home.

He lived in a dilapidated trailer, nine blocks from the school, with his older brother, twelve, and his two sisters, ten and seven. As we carefully climbed onto the wooden steps leading to the front door, we saw that the front door didn't latch and the screen door hung from the upper hinge. There was a trash bag covering one of the windows at the end of the trailer, which I believed was a bedroom. A rancid aroma of rotting trash and dirty clothing gushed out through a missing window in the front door. As we knocked, we heard several voices and children scrambling. An eerie silence settled as we knocked a second time. We waited.

Nancy called out: "Hello, is anyone home?"

After more silence, and what sounded like boxes being moved, the door opened just a little and another gush of thick, eye-watering air hit us in the face. Elizabeth, ten, peered through the crack in the opening, and quietly said, "Sorry, momma is sleeping." Then, she noticed her little brother standing with us and opened the door.

What we saw in the living room was heartbreaking. It is very hard to talk about it without tears even to this day. Lying in the middle of the room, on a mattress, was the children's mother. She appeared to be very sick. Stacks of clothes covered what furniture there was. In one corner stood a bedraggled Christmas tree that had many odd-looking, homemade decorations. Yes, Christmas was just a few weeks away. Beside her bed was a single metal folding chair. The children surrounded her with protective-looking stances and wide, nervous glances.

We realized that this was the first time anyone had been in their home for months; the first time since their mother had been diagnosed with terminal breast cancer. The oldest brother and sister began to tell us that they were taking care of their mom, and that she was going to be okay. The two younger children asked if we were going to take them away to an orphanage. Tears flowed as their mom began to carefully tell the story of what had led up to this. She was apprehensive at first, and gathered her children close as we shared with her that we were not there to separate them.

The room filled with tearful emotions as mom finally understood that our visit was an answer to her prayers. She knew that her time with her children was drawing to a close; actually just four months away. She begged that we help ensure that her children not be separated. She had no local family, or for that matter, anywhere in the state of Texas. She shared that she did have a brother in Washington State.

What transpired next was truly amazing. We made several phone calls to teachers, pastors, and friends, and within a few hours, an army of people from several churches in our city

Chapter Eleven

began to arrive. Carefully and respectfully tiptoeing through the home, clothes, and bedding were picked up and taken to the laundromat. The kitchen and refrigerator were cleaned, and filled with easy-to-cook food. Beds were changed. The front door was repaired along with several windows. After a few days, a local who owned rental houses opened a home for them to move into since the trailer was truly unlivable.

The children's uncle in Washington was contacted. He came to help. He stayed with them in their home and took care of his sister. Each day a home care nurse came to take care of her and to make sure that the children were coping. Throughout the entire time, the local churches and schools stood by assisting wherever possible. What seemed like an eternity, as the days and weeks passed, the children's mom grew weaker. Then, it was as if time stood still. I remember standing in the back yard, outside their home with the oldest children, who with an uncanny resilience, talked about what would come next. They knew time was short, and that they would be taken away from each other.

Earlier that week their uncle and his wife made the decision to take all four children to Washington to live with them. They mentioned it to the children's mom who found peace in knowing that they would be with family. The couple spent the next few days working out all the details before they informed the children. Everyone was called into mom's bedroom, and the news became known to all.

There wasn't a dry eye to be found. Nancy and I were so moved and blessed as we remembered the first time we met this family. We found out a little later that the school counselor was going to call social services the day after our sons brought the little boy to our home. She was going to remove the children from their mother because of the her concerns over the situation. Thank God we were called by Him to this family first.

Here again is why we, as children's pastors, senior pastors, and churches, need to be involved in reaching out to our local schools. This family would have slipped through the cracks of the system with great heartache, and who knows what lasting impact it would have on these children.

It will likely be easier for you to understand why, since moving to Fort Worth, eleven years ago, one of the main thrusts of our ministry has been to become a vital part of the local school district. Our first week, we visited Poynter Elementary just a couple of blocks from our church. It was an interesting visit as we walked onto the campus of this struggling, underprivileged school. Back then, the school didn't know how to handle a church wanting to come and assist them in their monumental task: the education of hundreds of children from our community. It took over a year of constant visits and lots of prayer for Poynter Elementary to completely open up to us. We had to earn their trust.

Sadly, over the years, the American church has not always been the most trustworthy entity when it comes to our schools. Often, the church has been harsh, judgmental, and unable to bend or understand the needs of local teachers and school officials, leaving both local schools and churches frustrated and in limbo.

Let me give an example. Last year, a school in a nearby school district, seeing their enormous needs, invited many faith-based groups to a well-catered breakfast and a tour of their school. The principal, in an emotionally-charged speech, shared the issues and needs they faced every day with the ever-changing demographics of today's students. They struggled not only to teach, but to try to meet the everyday needs of their students. Dozens of homeless students attended this school, as well as children from broken homes and angry children who had been used, abused, bullied, and/or ignored by almost every person in their lives. The principal's voice broke

Chapter Eleven

as he shared his own personal story, which in turn spurred on his deep desire to help his students succeed in life.

At the end of the presentation, he opened up the floor to anyone from the church groups who were present. One pastor stood and elegantly shared his desire to help but his church was already overwhelmed with community affairs. Another pastor shared their own plight of not having enough people to volunteer. Another church representative totally disagreed with the open door being offered to "the church," stating that there were laws against it. He didn't want to put his ministry in jeopardy to send parishioners into the school, but he did promise to pray for the principal and his needs. Last, a well-spoken minister, who came with his associate pastor, stood and offered their help as long as they could first be allowed to share the gospel with each child and with the teachers. We sat looking over this well-groomed group of pastors, and felt at a loss.

The face of the school principal said it all. He knew he was not going to get what he needed from the church leaders in his community. Then, we stood and said that we would love to help wherever and whenever needed. As other church groups left, we approached the principal. We shared what we were doing twenty miles away at our community school and his countenance began to change. He took us on a second, short trip around the most needed areas of his school, sharing a few individual stories of hurting children (no names of course), and where our resources and abilities would be of greatest value. We left there feeling that we had been given yet another incredible opportunity to touch the lives of both teachers and students in a whole new area.

Sadly, that was the last time we heard from this school. We called numerous times, even visited the school twice within the next month, and could not get a meeting with the principal.

What happened? I believe disappointment and frustration

set in that morning during the breakfast, and this man saw a brick wall between the school and the local churches. To this day, we pray for this school, in faith, believing that this wall will be knocked down, and the doors will open wide once again for the church to partner with the schools in that community.

To say that it is easy to cross the line and become partners with the schools would be untrue. It's not easy. It takes a lot of prayer, perseverance, and presence.

Today, our local school, Poynter Elementary, with whom we have partnered for over a decade, is an exemplary school with an amazing staff of dedicated teachers and leaders. From the school superintendent down, there is an open opportunity for faith-based groups to make the school district stronger.

So, how can you get involved with your local school?

What are some of the things that you, as a children's pastor or as a church can do to bless your local school district?

Here is what we are doing in our school district. We pray for them every day. We also pray *in* the schools.

I know what you are thinking: can pastors really do that? Yes, you can. We have taken teams of up to fifty intercessors from our church into two elementary schools on Saturday mornings to pray in every classroom, hallway, and bathroom. (It is a known fact that the greatest percentage of bullying takes place in the bathrooms.) We pray for each teacher, school employee, and specifically the principal and his or her staff. We have received several new requests to pray in local schools, and we fill these requests with gusto.

Does it change anything? Absolutely. There is a renewed peace in the classrooms, and teachers feel the results in the attention spans of their children.

We are active in all school activities throughout the year. We hold an after-school Bible club every Tuesday with an average of eighty plus students in attendance, called Kids Beach Club (KBC). This program has opened up so many

Chapter Eleven

incredible opportunities for our church to reach out to our schools and support the teachers. Through KBC, we have gained many new families who have joined our church; once, seventeen children made Jesus their "forever friend."

We honor thirty students every month with gift bags filled with goodies, something to read, something to wear, something to eat, and something to share. In each bag, we also include the greatest toy ever made—a brand new fuzzy tennis ball! We do this at another school every month for intermediate students.

We are involved with *Mathoween* and *Read-a-thons*, and in so many other opportunities. We accept all invitations to be involved in our local school. These invitations are incredible gifts from God.

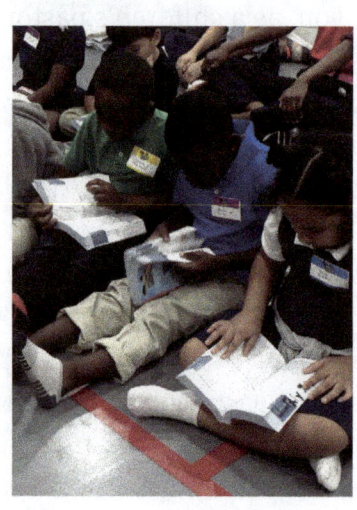

Our after-school KBC reading.

We have trained men and women called *All-Pro Dads and Moms* who assist every day at the school. These men and women are also Prayer Warriors, who, while serving in numerous areas, also walk the halls interceding for "our school." This is done at the request of the school and has proven to be amazingly successful. Once, we hosted a beautiful, appreciation dinner for the entire school from the principal down to the custodians. Special gift bags were presented to each teacher and staff member.

Today's schools have changed so much. To quote our Poynter Principal: "I have to be a counselor long before I can be a teacher anymore." Why? Today, children come to school with the world on their shoulders. They have chronic illnesses, long-standing syndromes, hang-ups, severe trust issues, fears, anxieties, and deep hurts. They are often hungry, sleep deprived, bullied, and scared. They have grown up long before their time. For instance, not long ago an educator came to me quite concerned about the changes in today's children. She tearfully shared that earlier that day she was certain she had experienced a demon in one of her kindergarten students.

Val Prather, Beach Club Volunteer Story Teacher, interacting with the students.

What do you do with that? Pray, I say. Pray earnestly. Continue to pray and lift up the schools in your area. They need you. They need what you have to offer. They need the hope and encouragement that comes from knowing there is someone out there who cares and supports them.

Over the years of our involvement in the community and the schools, our church has added many new families from our local school districts. It's been a particular blessing for me, personally, to officiate the baptisms of so many of these new faces, both the children and the adults.

One time, Nancy and I visited a Braum's restaurant with some friends in Tyler, Texas, where, more than ten years earlier, we had served as children's pastors. While eating a cheese burger, one of the Braum's employees approached Nancy with a huge smile.

"Are you Mrs. Baldwin?"

"Yes, I am."

This employee almost teared up as she explained that she had been in our story time in second and third grade at Whitehouse Elementary so many years ago. She continued to tell us that the highlight of her childhood had been the

Chapter Eleven

stories we shared.

Then she asked, "Where's Much, the purple puppet?" Before returning to work, she told us that she was now tells our stories to her own children!

If you want to change lives in your community, take that incredible step of faith and start new, amazing adventures in your local schools. The Lord will bless your efforts as you take these steps to change the world one child at a time!

Testimony of Brenda MacIntosh
A Parent's Perspective

I served as a children's church adult volunteer in the *Kidz-Turn* program for almost ten years, from 2009- 2018. This program had a profound effect on my family. The program provided structure, support and mentoring. We found a community and shared vision while serving with Pastors Ray and Nancy Baldwin. It is true that you can find your community through service.

We came into the program when my son turned seven. He was transitioning from a smaller classroom and this new program seemed big and a little scary. We decided to attend the services with him until he felt comfortable enough to attend on his own. During this period, God told my husband that the program needed help and that he was to serve there. It wasn't long before he was serving in lights, sound and tech support. I continued to serve in the program as well, accepting more responsibilities. This was the beginning of our service in children's ministry.

The *Kidz-Turn* program gave my family an opportunity to serve our church. If the *Kidz-Turn* was having a service, we were there. We became steady and familiar faces to the children and parents who attended the church. The *Kidz-Turn* ministry relied on volunteers. Weekly services, special events, worship rehearsals, and ministry trips required a committed team. The children in the program have benefited from adults that are dependable and committed to their good. This commitment to the program and the shared mission gave space for a loving community to develop.

As a parent volunteer, I appreciated the opportunity to grow as a mother and as a woman in ministry. This program challenged me in ways that I would never have sought out on my own. I benefited from the wisdom of experienced parents that had older children. I was able to share my own experiences with other parents. I was able to pray with children and parents over our shared difficulties and our joys. My own limits were tested during summer camps, survival campouts, and missions' trips. It was the weekly services that provided a framework for our relationships to grow. This framework allowed us to overcome challenges that would have seemed impossible without a shared vision.

Our children grew up in this program. The benefit to them and to our family is difficult to quantify. Our children developed a strong sense of service and sense of responsibility to the church. They both learned musical instruments, how to sing and to have no fear of the microphone. They are leaders who continue to seek out God in their personal lives. They share the gospel with friends and in our new church home in Denver, Colorado. The *Kidz-Turn* program established them in the Kingdom of God. What more could I ask?

— **Brenda MacIntosh**

Chapter Eleven

BEGIN THE CHANGE NOW

If you are a children's minister, we strongly encourage you to pick up the telephone and call the principal of the school closest to your church, or better still, arrange for a meet-and-greet with the principal. You may want to use some of the partnerships we have described in this chapter as your first plans to help the school. Later, we know you and your partner school will address new needs with fresh, exciting programs. As you work, share your progress in newsletters or magazines at your church. You could also share your successes at City Council meetings.

Please write to us as well. We want to share your joys and your life-changing experiences. Also, build missions trips for your children's ministry. These trips will create lifelong bonds.

If you are a parent, contact your children's minister, and ask how you can assist in the programs they are creating to benefit local schools. You could also volunteer to host a dinner with other church parents to not only discuss how they can minister to their children at home, but how they can become involved in the school-partnering ministry at your church. At home, share your testimony of how you became a Christian with your children.

We pray that the words in this book have inspired you to start where you are with what you have. We can't wait to see what God will do, through you to change the world one child at a time.

NOTES

1. Montrose J. Moses, *Children's Books and Reading* (New York: Mitchell Kennerley, 1907) 103.
2. Cathy Nutbrown, Peater Clough, and Philip Selbie, *Early Childhood Education: History, Philosphy and Expereince* (SAGE Publications, 2008) 154.
3. Elmer L. Towns, "History of Sunday School" in *Town's Sunday School Encyclopedia* (Illinois, Tyndale House Publisher, 1993).
4. Charles H. Spurgeon, "Jesus and the Children" (sermon, *Metropolitan Tabernacle Pulpit*, Newington: Metropolitan Tabernacle, October 17, 1886). https://www.spurgeon.org/wp-content/uploads/2020/03/51_Jesus_and_the_Children.pdf.

    Quote heard during a lecture on Church History at the River of Life Bible College and Theological Seminary.
5. Harry Sprange, *Children in Revival: 300 Years of God's Work in Scotland* (Scotland: Christian Focus Publications, 2002).
6. Ibid.
7. Ibid.
8. Ibid.
9. Ibid.
10. Article attributed to the TPCTimes Magazine, TPC's monthly magazine.

Notes

11   Quote attributed to Maya Angelou, the late African-American author and poet.
12   "When Do Americans Become Christian?" in *Holiness Today* (Kansas, The Church of the Nazarene, November 2017). https://www.holinesstoday.org/when-do-americans-become-christian.

   The article cites a survey by the International Bible Society.
13   Becky Fischer, "There's A Children's Revival Coming!" in Kids In Ministry International (August 24, 2016). https://kidsinministry.org/18-kids-get-saved-wv-school/
14   Quote attributed to Henry Ford.
15   *Wikipedia, The Free Encyclopedia*, s.v. "Single Parents in the United States," https://en.wikipedia.org/wiki/Single_parents_in_the_United_States.

   Information according to a report released by the United States Census Bureau, "Custodial Mothers and Fathers and Their Child Support: 2015."
16   *Wikipedia, The Free Encyclopedia*, s.v. "Marriage and Divorce Rates in the US, 1990–2007," https://en.wikipedia.org/wiki/Divorce_in_the_United_States#/media/File:Marriage_and_Divorce_Rates_in_the_US_1990-2007.png.

   According to Sally C. Curtin and Paul D. Sutton in "Marriage Rates in the United States, 1900–2018," marriage rates have dropped to as low as 6.5 per thousand (NCHS Health E-State, https://www.cdc.gov/nchs/data/hestat/marriage_rate_2018/marriage_rate_2018.htm).
17   Ibid.
18   "Child Poverty," in National Center for Children in Poverty, *Bank Street Graduate School of Education*. http://stage.nccp.org/topics/childpoverty.html.
19   Ibid.
20   Ibid.
21   Ibid.

Pastor Ray Baldwin
Children's Pastor

& Nancy Baldwin

ABOUT THE AUTHORS

Ray and Nancy Baldwin have served as children's pastors for over forty years.

Ray was born and raised in England. He has lived in the United States since 1976. He served as a senior pastor in Iowa for ten years, during which he and his wife, Nancy, created *SureWord Children's Ministries*. Ray met Jesus in a small Nazarene Church in Manchester, England, in 1971, at the age of nineteen. He attended college at Nazarene Theological College, where he met Nancy, who studied there as well. They married in Manchester in 1975.

Ray has written dozens of exciting stories for children called, *The Brickbach Bunch*, all based on his adventures and experiences as a child growing up in northern England. He taught a course in children's ministries at River of Life Bible School in Rusk, Texas, and was a team member to develop a children's ministry course for SUM Bible College and Theological Seminary in 2018.

Nancy was born in Chariton, Iowa, and moved to England to attend college. Nancy and Ray wrote and produced the popular video teaching resource material, *Choices*, in 1984. It is used in schools around the United States. While they served as children's pastors at Good News Church in Yukon, Oklahoma.

Ray and Nancy have two sons, Austin and Geoffrey. Today,

Chapter Eleven

their sons and their wives are involved in StrikeForce. Over their forty years of ministry, the Baldwins have traveled extensively with StrikeForce Ministry Teams and the Knights of God, preaching and teaching in churches, seminars, and conferences in the United States, Mexico, Australia, England, and Europe. Both Ray and Nancy are accomplished musicians, singers, puppeteers, and storytellers.

Ray and Nancy currently serve as the children's pastors at *Turning*Point Church in Fort Worth, Texas. To contact Pastors Ray and Nancy, please email them at praynan@aol.com.

E

F P

T O Z

L P E D

P E C F D

E D F C Z P

F E L O P Z D

D E F P O T E C

L E F O D P C T

F D P L T C E O